OPPOSING
VIEWPOINTS®
SERIES

| Violence

Other Books of Related Interest:

Opposing Viewpoints Series

America's Youth

Domestic Violence

Gun Violence

At Issues Series

How Can School Violence Be Prevented?

How Can Domestic Violence Be Prevented?

How Can Gang Violence Be Prevented?

Is Media Violence a Problem?

School Shootings

Video Games

Current Controversies Series

Child Abuse

School Violence

Violence Against Women

"Congress shall make
no law . . . abridging
the freedom of speech,
or of the press."

First Amendment to the U.S. Constitution

The basic foundation of our democracy is the First Amendment guarantee of freedom of expression. The Opposing Viewpoints series is dedicated to the concept of this basic freedom and the idea that it is more important to practice it than to enshrine it.

Violence

Louise Gerdes, Book Editor

GREENHAVEN PRESS

An imprint of Thomson Gale, a part of The Thomson Corporation

THOMSON
™
GALE

Detroit • New York • San Francisco • New Haven, Conn. • Waterville, Maine • London

Christine Nasso, *Publisher*
Elizabeth Des Chenes, *Managing Editor*

© 2008 The Gale Group.

Star logo is a trademark and Gale and Greenhaven Press are registered trademarks used herein under license.

For more information, contact:
Greenhaven Press
27500 Drake Rd.
Farmington Hills, MI 48331-3535
Or you can visit our Internet site at http://www.gale.com

LIBRARY OF CONGRESS CATALOGING-IN-PUBLICATION DATA

Violence / Louise Gerdes, book editor.
    p. cm. -- Opposing Viewpoints
    Includes bibliographical references and index.
    ISBN-13: 978-0-7377-3364-8 (hardcover)
    ISBN-13: 978-0-7377-3365-5 (pbk.)
    1. Violence--Juvenile literature. 2. Aggressiveness--Juvenile literature. I. Gerdes,
Louise I., 1953-
    HM1116.V52 2008
    303.60973--dc22
                                                                    2007029808

ISBN-10: 0-7377-3364-0
ISBN-10: 0-7377-3365-9

Printed in the United States of America
10 9 8 7 6 5 4 3 2 1

Contents

Chapter 3: What Factors Lead to Youth Violence?

Chapter 4: How Should Society Respond to Violence?

Why Consider Opposing Viewpoints?

> "*The only way in which a human being can make some approach to knowing the whole of a subject is by hearing what can be said about it by persons of every variety of opinion and studying all modes in which it can be looked at by every character of mind. No wise man ever acquired his wisdom in any mode but this.*"
>
> *John Stuart Mill*

In our media-intensive culture it is not difficult to find differing opinions. Thousands of newspapers and magazines and dozens of radio and television talk shows resound with differing points of view. The difficulty lies in deciding which opinion to agree with and which "experts" seem the most credible. The more inundated we become with differing opinions and claims, the more essential it is to hone critical reading and thinking skills to evaluate these ideas. Opposing Viewpoints books address this problem directly by presenting stimulating debates that can be used to enhance and teach these skills. The varied opinions contained in each book examine many different aspects of a single issue. While examining these conveniently edited opposing views, readers can develop critical thinking skills such as the ability to compare and contrast authors' credibility, facts, argumentation styles, use of persuasive techniques, and other stylistic tools. In short, the Opposing Viewpoints series is an ideal way to attain the higher-level thinking and reading skills so essential in a culture of diverse and contradictory opinions.

In addition to providing a tool for critical thinking, Opposing Viewpoints books challenge readers to question their own strongly held opinions and assumptions. Most people form their opinions on the basis of upbringing, peer pressure, and personal, cultural, or professional bias. By reading carefully balanced opposing views, readers must directly confront new ideas as well as the opinions of those with whom they disagree. This is not to simplistically argue that everyone who reads opposing views will—or should—change his or her opinion. Instead, the series enhances readers' understanding of their own views by encouraging confrontation with opposing ideas. Careful examination of others' views can lead to the readers' understanding of the logical inconsistencies in their own opinions, perspective on why they hold an opinion, and the consideration of the possibility that their opinion requires further evaluation.

Evaluating Other Opinions

To ensure that this type of examination occurs, Opposing Viewpoints books present all types of opinions. Prominent spokespeople on different sides of each issue as well as well-known professionals from many disciplines challenge the reader. An additional goal of the series is to provide a forum for other, less-known, or even unpopular viewpoints. The opinion of an ordinary person who has had to make the decision to cut off life support from a terminally ill relative, for example, may be just as valuable and provide just as much insight as a medical ethicist's professional opinion. The editors have two additional purposes in including these less-known views. One, the editors encourage readers to respect others' opinions—even when not enhanced by professional credibility. It is only by reading or listening to and objectively evaluating others' ideas that one can determine whether they are worthy of consideration. Two, the inclusion of such viewpoints encourages the important critical thinking skill of objectively evaluating an author's credentials and bias. This evaluation will illuminate an author's reasons for taking a particular stance on an issue and will aid in readers' evaluation of the author's ideas.

It is our hope that these books will give readers a deeper understanding of the issues debated and an appreciation of the complexity of even seemingly simple issues when good and honest people disagree. This awareness is particularly important in a democratic society such as ours in which people enter into public debate to determine the common good. Those with whom one disagrees should not be regarded as enemies but rather as people whose views deserve careful examination and may shed light on one's own.

Thomas Jefferson once said that "difference of opinion leads to inquiry, and inquiry to truth." Jefferson, a broadly educated man, argued that "if a nation expects to be ignorant and free . . . it expects what never was and never will be." As individuals and as a nation, it is imperative that we consider the opinions of others and examine them with skill and discernment. The Opposing Viewpoints series is intended to help readers achieve this goal.

David L. Bender and Bruno Leone,
Founders

> "*Something is wrong when thirty-two people die from gun violence inflicted by others, not just at Virginia Tech on April 16, but every day in this country.*"
>
> *Paul Helmke, president of the Brady Campaign to Prevent Gun Violence.*

> "*All that seems to be on the minds of many in the media and at the offices of gun control extremists is figuring out how to exploit this horrible tragedy to erode and eventually destroy the right, and the means, of self-defense.*"
>
> *Alan Gottlieb, founder of the Second Amendment Foundation.*

Introduction

Almost as soon as the media broadcast news of the tragic shooting at Virginia Tech on April 16, 2007, commentators began to debate what could have prevented the deaths of thirty-two students and teachers at the Blacksburg, Virginia, school. One of the perennial debates that inevitably follow a school shooting is whether gun control might have prevented the tragedy. Indeed, gun control remains one of the most hotly contested issues in the United States, a nation with not only one of the highest rates of civilian gun ownership but also one of the highest rates of gun-related injuries and deaths among the world's industrialized nations. One question raised following the Virginia Tech shooting is whether laws should make it more difficult for a person with a history of mental illness to obtain a gun.

In the early months of 2007, Korean-born Seung-Hui Cho, the Virginia Tech shooter, purchased a .22-caliber Walther P-22, a 9mm Glock, and fifty rounds of ammunition. Cho presented his Virginia driver's license, his checkbook, and his immigration card—identification sufficient to complete the required federal background check for handgun purchases. There was no information in the federal database to disallow the sale. There was no reason for the gun dealers to suspect that for years Cho had exhibited bizarre and aggressive behavior that had troubled Cho's parents, peers, and teachers. Nor did the database reveal that in December 2005 a Virginia judge ordered Cho to receive outpatient psychiatric treatment, having found Cho to be "an imminent danger to himself." The Gun Control Act of 1968 prohibits possession of a firearm by anyone "adjudicated as a mental defective." The federal law defines a "mental defective" as a person who "is a danger to himself or others." The regulations broadly define adjudication to include "a determination by a court, board, commission or other lawful authority." Thus, federal law would have disqualified Cho from buying a handgun. However, Virginia authorities did not put Judge Paul Barnett's order into the federal background-check system because Virginia law requires commitment to a mental hospital to prevent an applicant from buying a gun.

The public outrage that followed the Virginia Tech shooting spurred Congress to consider legislation that would give states incentives to plug gaps between state and federal laws. Supporters claim that these gaps made Cho's killing spree possible. Paul Helmke, president of the Brady Campaign to Prevent Gun Violence, argues that Cho was able to buy the weapons because of "lethal loopholes" in the background-check system. A May 2007 report of the pro-gun control group Third Way reveals that only twenty-two states provide any mental records into the system, "rendering . . . the [federal] law useless in most states." The proposed bill would indeed clarify, tighten, and fund current laws on state participation in the National Instant Criminal Background Check System (NICS).

The National Rifle Association (NRA), an organization that generally opposes most limits on the right of American citizens to own guns, supports the legislation. "We've been on record for decades that records of those adjudicated as mentally defective and deemed to be a danger to others or to themselves should be part of the national instant-check system and not be allowed to own a firearm," claims NRA spokesman Andrew Arulanandam. "The mental health lobby and the medical lobby are the impediments—they are against release of records," Arulanandam maintains.

Mental health groups do, in truth, caution against overly broad labels that identify mental illness as an indicator of potential violence. "It's very easy and very tempting when something as horrible as Virginia Tech occurs to assume that mental illness correlates with a propensity for violence," argues Ron Honberg, director of policy and legal affairs for the National Alliance on Mental Illness. According to Honberg, however, "that's not borne out for the majority of people with mental illness." Many of those who may once have been mentally disabled "have gone on to recover and are living independently and are working and are upstanding citizens." Widespread reporting, opponents argue, could also lead to discrimination that might deter people from seeking treatment. "We have real grave concerns about people with mental illness being a population that's singled out," Honberg claims.

Those who support gun ownership also oppose efforts to promote increased reporting, but for different reasons. Gun Owners of America (GOA), for example, opposes strengthening NICS because it believes the system is both ineffective and intrusive. "All the background checks in the world will not stop bad guys from getting firearms," GOA claims. The key to reducing gun violence, gun advocates argue, is to increase penalties against criminals who use guns, not restrict the constitutional right of Americans to use firearms in hunting, sport shooting, and self-defense. "The [Virginia Tech] shooting demands an immediate end to the gun-free-zone law, which leaves the nation's schools at the mercy of madmen," asserts Larry Pratt, GOA executive director.

Debates over what policies will best prevent horrific tragedies such as the mass murder at Virginia Tech remain hotly contested. The authors of the viewpoints in *Opposing Viewpoints: Violence* explore these and other issues concerning the nature and scope of violence in the following chapters: Is Violence a Serious Problem? What Factors Contribute to Human Violence? What Factors Lead to Youth Violence? and How Should Society Respond to Violence?

Is Violence
a Serious Problem?

Chapter Preface

In October 1998 Matthew Shepard, a twenty-one-year-old gay student at the University of Wyoming, was lured from a bar, tied to a wooden ranch fence, and beaten into unconsciousness. He died the next week. Public outrage over what many labeled a hate crime led to calls for federal intervention. Hate crimes are generally defined as crimes that were motivated by bias against a social group, including those identifiable by race, religion, sexual orientation, disability, ethnicity, nationality, age, gender, or political affiliation. Included groups vary among state laws. Federal law has since 1969 prohibited hate crimes against individuals in identified groups trying to engage in federally protected activities such as voting. In 1994 Congress increased the penalties and expanded the social groups represented. Controversy in the early 2000s surrounds attempts to drop the requirement that the victim be engaging in a federally protected activity, making many hate crimes a federal offense. These efforts have fueled one of the enduring controversies in the hate crime debate—whether hate crimes merit federal intervention. Some commentators contend that hate crimes are a growing problem that threatens U.S. society. Other observers assert that labeling violent acts hate crimes is redundant and dangerous.

Those who argue that federal intercession is necessary assert that the number of hate crimes is increasing and that victims of such crimes are more likely to suffer physical violence. "Hate crimes and arsons are increasing," claim civil rights activists Karen McGill Lawson and Wade Henderson. Such crimes, the authors argue, "injure or even kill thousands of people, terrify countless others, divide Americans against each other, and distort our entire society." What is more, the authors claim, "hate crimes are much more likely than other crimes to be acts of brutal violence." The victim of a hate crime, they maintain, "is more likely to be severely injured in body, and in spirit as well, than the victim of an ordinary offense." Senator Gordon Smith and like-minded lawmakers agree. They argue that the government has a duty to protect citizens from such crimes. "A principal responsibility of government is to protect and defend its citizens and to come to the aid of the mistreated. As a nation founded on the ideals of tolerance and justice, we simply cannot accept violence that is motivated by bias and hate," Smith claims.

Critics Disagree

Critics of hate crime laws disagree. "Hate is a vague, complex, and highly personal emotion and does not pertain to a particular set of beliefs. Thus, labeling violent acts committed against certain victims as 'hate crimes' is deeply problematic," claims conservative analyst Andrew Sullivan. In fact, he argues, "'Equal opportunity' crimes such as random acts of violence pose a bigger threat to society. They occur much more frequently than hate crimes, are no less brutal, and threaten the safety of entire communities, not just particular groups." Libertarian Jacob Sullum agrees. "It's not a stretch to say that hate crime laws, by their very nature, punish people for their opinions," he suggests. Critics reason, for example, that hate crimes punish a person who assaults someone because they disapprove of their religion more severely than one who assaults a random victim. Federal hate-crime legislation "continues the unfortunate tendency to federalize crimes that are properly the business of state and local governments, just so legislators . . . can show they care," Sullum concludes.

Whether hate crime is a serious problem that merits federal protection remains contentious. The authors in the following chapter present their views in answer to the question, Is Violence a Serious Problem?

"The impact of violent crime is far-reaching."

Violent Crime Is a Serious Problem

Mary Lou Leary

Violent crime has a significant impact on victims and communities, argues Mary Lou Leary in the following viewpoint. Victims not only experience the immediate physical, emotional, and financial trauma of violent crime, but they also suffer less obvious damages, she maintains. The marriages of parents who lose a child to homicide, Leary claims for example, are often broken or damaged. The impact of violent crime on America's youth, she asserts, is also alarming. Teen victimization is linked to substance abuse and teen victims are more likely to commit violent crimes themselves. Leary is executive director of the victims rights organization, National Center for Victims of Crime.

As you read, consider the following questions:

1. According to the Bureau of Justice Statistics, how much do victims of violent crime lose annually?

Mary Lou Leary, "The Cost of Crime: Understanding the Financial and Human Impact of Criminal Activity," *Testimony of Mary Lou Leary, executive director, National Center for Victims of Crime, before the Committee on the Judiciary, United States Senate,* September 19, 2006. Reproduced by permission of the author.

2. In Leary's opinion, how long can some violent crime victims suffer posttraumatic stress disorder?

3. In the author's view, why do some homicide survivors struggle to maintain their careers?

We know crime results in significant out-of-pocket losses to victims—the Bureau of Justice Statistics estimates over $1.14 billion in annual losses to victims of violent crime, and another $15 billion to victims of property crime. The Federal Trade Commission estimates that losses from identity theft alone total $5 billion a year.

The Intangible Costs of Crime

Medical costs, funeral costs, lost wages, and other tangible out-of-pocket costs impose a significant burden on victims. Those of us who work with crime victims know the intangible costs of crime can be even greater. We witness how victimization often leads to increased substance abuse, higher rates of depression and posttraumatic stress disorder, increased risk of suicide, homelessness, higher rates of unemployment and underemployment, and negative long-term health consequences. The impact can be physical, emotional, financial, and social. Crime affects more than just the immediate victim. It reaches family, friends, schoolmates, co-workers, and communities.

Victims of violent crime are particularly at risk of developing posttraumatic stress disorder (PTSD). Nearly 50 percent of rape victims, 37 percent of stalking victims, 32 percent of physical assault victims, 15 percent of shooting or stabbing victims, and 7 percent of witnesses to violence will develop PTSD. PTSD has a profound effect on a victim's quality of life and ability to function. A person with PTSD may experience disturbing flashbacks or other episodes of reliving the event. They often become adept at avoiding anything—people, places, or things—that could remind them of the traumatic experience. They may become emotionally paralyzed—often through

Violence in America

America may be the most violent country in the world when compared to other industrialized nations. Violence is deeply rooted in American society, and has become woven into the fabric of American lifestyle. Violence invades our intimate relationships, our schools, and our work environments.

Christine Bude, Associated Content,
December 28, 2006.

substance abuse—in order to avoid painful, overwhelming feelings. They may also show symptoms of psychological and physiological arousal, such as being very jumpy, easily startled, or irritable. They may find themselves constantly on guard and may have difficulty concentrating or sleeping. Without treatment, many people continue to suffer symptoms of PTSD up to 10 years after the traumatic event.

The Impact on Teens

Moreover, we are just beginning to understand the cost of crime to our nation's youth. *Our Vulnerable Teenagers*, a landmark report released in 2002 by the National Center for Victims of Crime and the National Council on Crime and Delinquency, documented the far-reaching impact of victimization at this crucial point in human development: victimized youth (ages 12 to 19) report more truancy, more negative contact with teachers, and increased conflict with other students, all of which can disrupt educational performance and impede later career prospects. The link between teen victimization and substance abuse, teen pregnancy, and eating disorders has also been well-established.

One of the most alarming impacts of crime on teens is the strong relationship between being a victim of crime and committing criminal offenses. Being a victim of crime has been identified as the strongest predictor of violent offending among our nation's youth.

On an individual level, victims and those who serve them can tell you more about the true cost of crime, and it goes far beyond dollars. At the National Center, we hear these stories every day from victims who call our National Crime Victim Helpline.

The Impact of Homicide

When we think of the impact of crime, the first image that often comes to mind are survivors of homicide victims. While no one can fully understand what a homicide survivor goes through, all of us . . . empathize with what it must feel like to learn of the violent death of a loved one. We can appreciate that the family suffers shock and unbearable grief. But there are other dramatic effects that many of us may not have considered.

Time and again, we hear of marriages broken up in the aftermath of murder, especially after parents lose a child to homicide. Husbands and wives may withdraw from each other and may deal with the tragedy in very unique, and sometimes conflicting, ways. One parent may appear to recover fairly quickly while the other can't stop crying months later. One may be focused on the criminal justice system response and being present at every court proceeding; the other may feel that no matter what happens in the courts, it doesn't matter because it will not bring the loved one back. In some cases, blame and guilt may drive a wedge between parents of a murdered child.

Survivors of homicide may also struggle with maintaining their careers. Many survivors are simply not ready to return to their "normal" routine soon after the tragedy and need more than the typical two weeks of bereavement leave. Many survivors aren't even offered two weeks, and find they can't return to work in time to save their job.

In communities where there has been a homicide on the street, we hear from the survivors who daily walk past the bloodstained sidewalk where their loved one was killed. Few of us think about the fact that it can take days or weeks for blood to be cleaned up—if ever. Instead, that crime scene exacts a daily, emotional toll on the family members and friends left behind, the children and neighbors who see those bloodstains every day.

The Impact of Other Violent Crime

The impact of violent crime is far-reaching. We can picture the immediate hospitalization and treatment of an assault victim or battered spouse who has been beaten, burned, or slashed. But after discharge, what about the scars? We hear heartbreaking cases of permanent disfigurement, with victims unable to obtain the expensive reconstructive or cosmetic surgery that would give them the confidence to go out in public, to resume employment, or to date again.

But not all violent crime leaves a visible impact. One caller to our Helpline had been the victim of an attempted armed robbery when she was en route to make a deposit for her boss. The robbery was thwarted, and she sustained no physical injuries, but she was severely traumatized. She had believed she was about to die. She called us, saying that because of the robbery attempt, she hadn't left her apartment in over a year. She was severely depressed and had gained 100 pounds. She was calling because she was afraid her husband was going to divorce her and didn't know where else to turn.

Another recent caller had been held up at gunpoint at her retail job at a jewelry store. The recognized "cost" of that crime was the cost of the merchandise taken. But to that victim, the "cost" is with her every day. She has been terrified to go back to work at the same business, but knows that she wouldn't be able to make the same salary if she started over at another store. So she continues in that job, traumatized every time she goes to work.

Hidden Consequences

We heard from a rape victim who, in her efforts to avoid thinking about the rape has for several years gotten drunk before having sex with her husband. As a result, she has developed a substance abuse problem.

We heard from a victim of child sexual abuse, now in her late 20s, who Googled her name, bringing up court documents that detailed the sexual abuse and named her as the victim. She felt traumatized and exposed all over again.

Even the steps victims can take to promote their future safety often have unintended negative consequences. Women fleeing domestic violence or stalking may have to leave their job, their community, and their circle of friends to relocate to a safe place. To keep from being traced by a determined perpetrator, a woman might change her name and her Social Security number. Then she finds she no longer has any work or credit history. With a "clean slate" Social Security number, she's unable to get a job or even a volunteer position. She may have trouble registering her children at school. She often can't even get a library card. . . .

It is important, when we talk about the "cost of crime" to use dollar figures simply as a starting point. The real cost of crime includes the cost to individual quality of life and to society-at-large from the substance abuse, depression and PTSD, homelessness, loss of employment, poor school performance, and other consequences that drain our social system and keep people from leading secure and productive lives.

| "Crime in the U.S. is not on the rise. In fact it is falling dramatically and has been for years."

Violent Crime Is Decreasing

Tim Wise

Violent crime has been decreasing for decades, maintains Tim Wise in the following viewpoint, but not for the reasons tough-on-crime politicians claim. Strict state laws do not reduce violent crime, he argues. In fact, Wise claims, a majority of those incarcerated under strict laws are for nonviolent offenses. Policies that reduce extreme poverty and the marginalization of minorities will reduce violent crime, he asserts, not incarcerating more offenders. Wise, an antiracist activist, is author of White Like Me: Reflections on Race from a Privileged Son.

As you read, consider the following questions:

1. For what offense are a disproportionate number of new offenders incarcerated, in Wise's view?

2. According to the author, what have researchers found is a consequence of incarcerating youthful offenders?

3. How does the author explain the racial crime gaps in the United States?

Tim Wise, "A Quite Deliberate Failure: Reflections on the Politics of Crime," *Z Magazine*, April 01, 2004. Reproduced by permission.

Though it is always difficult to predict the outcome of an election in the United States, it is quite a bit easier to make accurate pronouncements about the way in which an election campaign will unfold. No matter the candidates, certain things are virtually guaranteed to happen: from nasty campaign ads that attack the personal integrity of one's opponent, to lavish spending by the major parties in order to sway the public to their candidate.

And this too: in every election cycle, one can fairly predict that the two major candidates for President will fall over themselves to prove to the voters that they are the toughest on crime; which remains one of the hottest of hot-button issues in the U.S.

Yet in truth there is little reason to believe that any candidate claiming to be tough on crime is serious. After all, they almost never seem to propose the kinds of policies that we know from the available evidence would actually reduce the incidence of criminal victimization. While politicians love to be tough on criminals, being tough on crime is an entirely different matter.

There are several problems with the anti-crime rhetoric we are likely to hear between now and the [next] election: among them, the reality that crime rates are much lower than believed and have dropped dramatically in recent years; the equal reality that lock-'em-up strategies favored by most politicians seeking votes are actually either ineffective or counterproductive to crime control efforts; and finally, that the only way to truly lower crime rates in the long run is to address the structural conditions that give rise to it in the first place: those "root causes" about which no one seems anxious to speak, for fear they be branded "bleeding hearts."

Problems with Anti-Crime Rhetoric

But in fact, without a comprehensive policy to confront glaring economic inequalities and the conditions of extreme poverty, crime will never be adequately attacked in the United States, meaning that it is the bleeding hearts, and not the crackdown crowd, who actually hold out the best hope for a safer nation.

Since political elites are not (by and large) stupid, and since they are regularly bombarded with the studies and data to indicate which anti-crime strategies work best, their continued unwillingness to engage root causes can only signify that they don't really want to make a serious long-term dent in crime, or at least that if they do, they would still prefer the political advantage offered by public fear: a fear they can masterfully exploit come election time. Given the political payoff of anti-crime fear-mongering (especially the overtly racist way in which such pandering has played out historically), there is little reason to expect things to change anytime soon.

The Truth About Crime in America

Fact is, although crime stories regularly top local news broadcasts, and crime as an issue always figures prominently in political campaigns, crime in the U.S. is not on the rise. In fact it is falling dramatically and has been for years. In urban centers, often viewed as havens for criminals (especially those of color), crime has been plummeting, and from 1991–1999 the murder rate in large cities dropped by over half.

Between 1993 and 2002, violent crime rates in the U.S. fell 54 percent, and by 2002, the nation's violent victimization rate had fallen to its lowest point since 1973: the year when victimization data began to be collected by the Justice Department. Even in raw number terms, crime has plummeted, with 23 million total criminal victimizations in 2002 (both violent and property crimes combined), compared to 44 million victimizations in 1973.

To these facts, naturally, the get-tough crowd has a ready answer. As [former] Attorney General John Ashcroft has argued, of course crime is down, but this, he says, is only because of tougher sentences, more police on the streets, and the hard-nosed conservative policies adopted in the past few decades, by Republicans and Democrats alike.

The Irony of the Lock-'em-Up Mentality

But get-tough policies are far less instrumental in reducing crime rates than the relative strength of the economy at any given moment. As indicated by cross-state crime comparisons, there is simply no positive relationship between the severity of a state's laws and decreases in murder, rape or assault: the three most serious violent crimes. Expanding a city's police force or prison capacity likewise has not been found to bear any positive relationship to reducing homicide rates. Also, since the majority of new incarcerations have been for non-violent offenses—disproportionately drug offenses—it makes little sense to credit the prison binge for declining crime rates: after all, those bearing the brunt of the lock-'em up policy are not violent offenders at all, let alone the worst of the worst.

What's more, the very crackdown policies that obviously can reduce crime in the short-run (by removing particular felons from the streets) can actually have a boomerang effect, thereby increasing crime overall. Researchers have found that incarceration of youthful offenders—a staple of the get-tough crowd that prefers prosecuting young criminals as adults—tends to delay the onset of delinquency cessation, and thereby increase the risk of future offending by these juveniles upon release.

Likewise, once an offender has a criminal record, their future prospects for employment and earnings fall dramatically, thereby increasing the likelihood of re-offending. Studies have found that those with criminal records have unemployment rates of nearly 50 percent, and that having a prison record reduces the amount of hours employed after one's release by 25–30 percent. In part, this is because so many employers—as

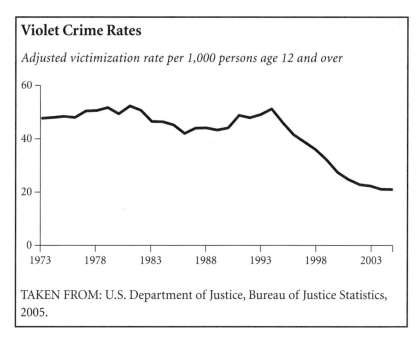

Violet Crime Rates

Adjusted victimization rate per 1,000 persons age 12 and over

TAKEN FROM: U.S. Department of Justice, Bureau of Justice Statistics, 2005.

many as 6 in 10 according to one study—openly admit that they would never knowingly hire an ex-offender.

So although the U.S. may be enjoying the short-term benefits of massive incarcerations, once the bulk of those offenders are released from prison (as most will be since they are not in for major crimes), their inability to find steady employment may only increase crime rates in the future. We may, in other words, reap what we have sown.

Poverty, Geography, and Living Conditions as the Key to Crime

Not only do politicians tend to support policies that make things worse, they rarely talk about the kinds of policies needed to make things substantially better, at least in the long term. Though it may be unpopular with many, the fact remains that the conditions of poverty and economic marginalization are the key factors driving violent crimes in the U.S., and only an amelioration of those conditions can hold out long-term and lasting hope for reducing the risk of victimization to the nation's people.

No, poverty does not cause crime itself, and yes, most poor folks don't commit crime. But that doesn't deny the link between economic destitution and criminality. After all, not everyone who smokes gets cancer—in fact, most probably won't—but no one seriously disputes the linkage between the two things. Likewise, not everyone who gets shot in the head dies: but only a fool would dispute the generally high correlation between those things either.

Those who dispute the link between poverty and crime tend to oversimplify the issue, by noting that there is no direct correlation between income levels and crime rates. Although this is true for the most part, it misses the point. It is not income per se, nor even poverty in the abstract, but certain conditions associated with severe poverty that are most highly linked to criminality. Thus, the racial crime gaps in the U.S.—whereby African Americans commit a disproportionate amount of violent street crimes (though whites continue to commit the majority)—is entirely the result of different conditions in which whites and blacks find themselves living.

Black Poverty Is Severe

Although whites suffer poverty too, black poverty is more severe and more likely to correlate with crime. Seven out of ten poor whites live in stable, mostly non-poor neighborhoods, while eighty-five percent of the black poor live in mostly poor areas. Blacks are three times more likely to live in extreme poverty than whites (less than half the poverty line) and six times more likely to live in concentrated poverty neighborhoods. Indeed, three-quarters of persons living in concentrated poverty neighborhoods are people of color.

Looking specifically at homicide rates, a study published in the *Journal of the American Medical Association* found that crowded housing was the key to higher murder rates among blacks in the U.S. When census tracts with similar incomes, population density and housing conditions are compared, racial murder rate differences evaporate, because the poorest neighborhoods have similar homicide rates, no matter their racial composition.

But rarely do politicians talk about confronting systemic resource deprivation in black and brown communities as a central feature, or even side feature, of their anti-crime platforms. Instead, they speak of more cops, more jails, and longer sentences, no matter how inadequate (and even counterproductive) such policies may in fact be. Nowhere is this more evident than with regard to drug crimes.

War on Drugs or Race War?

Although all available evidence suggests that whites are equally or more likely to use drugs than blacks or Latinos, and roughly equally likely to sell them, the fact remains that people of color continue to bear the brunt of the law enforcement crackdown which comprises the largest component of the so-called war on drugs.

For example, although white youth demonstrate greater usage of illegal narcotics than youth of color (SAMHSA, various), the juvenile justice system continues to treat youth of color as the biggest problem. Black youth arrested for a drug offense, with no prior records, are forty-eight times more likely to be incarcerated than their white counterparts, even when all other factors surrounding the arrest are similar. Although blacks and Latinos are 90 percent of persons incarcerated nationally for drugs, they represent only 23 percent of drug users according to the most recent federal data. Meanwhile, whites, who are between 70 percent and three-fourths of users, comprise less than ten percent of those incarcerated for drugs.

In all, black drug users are nearly twenty times more likely than anyone else to spend time in prison for their use, and in fifteen states, the rate of black incarceration for drug offenses is anywhere from 20–57 times greater than for whites, despite equal or greater rates of drug law violations by whites. Amazingly, when all other factors surrounding an arrest are the same, black cocaine offenders are twice as likely to be sent to prison and will serve, on average, forty months more than white offenders.

According to a Justice Department report from February 2001, police are more than twice as likely to search vehicles driven by blacks after pulling them over, even though whites, when searched, are more than twice as likely to be in possession of illegal items. Latino drivers were between 2 and 2.26 times more likely to be personally searched or to have their cars searched by police, even though they are less likely than blacks or whites, per capita, to use drugs and thus possess them at any given moment.

War on Drugs Makes Little Sense

In other words, the war on drugs is so completely focused on people of color—who statistically make up a small percentage of those committing drug offenses—that it makes little sense to consider it a war on drugs at all.

And to the extent said war focuses not on where the drugs are, but mostly where they are *not*, one must either conclude that policymakers and law enforcement agents who carry out this type of campaign are extraordinarily incapable of recognizing futility when they see it, or else that their main concern is not reducing drug use and abuse, but rather, controlling black and brown bodies. Given the history of quite deliberate social control of persons of color—which became harder to do overtly after the fall of segregation and Jim Crow, but which could be re-imposed by other means via mass incarceration in the present-day—the latter seems far more likely than the former.

After all, it was President [Bill] Clinton who buried the findings of a report his own White House commissioned from the RAND Corporation, which concluded that drug education and treatment strategies were up to five times more effective, and far less costly, than get-tough enforcement efforts. In other words, if elites wanted to stem drug abuse or drug related crimes they already know how to do it, yet they refuse to act on what they know, all rhetoric and feigned concern aside.

So this election season, let us both prepare for (and prepare to resist) political grandstanding on the issue of crime and public safety. As with terrorism, there is much to be gained in political terms from stoking public panic, facts be damned. And as with terrorism too, public policy that fails to make the American public any safer in their homes or on the street, nonetheless plays well to a cowed populace whose fear can be translated into votes for the guy who promises to best impersonate an Old West sheriff.

But just as those lawmen of old gained power from the existence of external threats to the public they ostensibly served, and just as they thrived on their role as "protectors and defenders" of all that was good and wholesome, so too do today's political elites need crime and disorder in order to justify their own power. However much they may personally wish for crime to decrease, one has to wonder how their political careers could withstand such a blow.

> *"Overall violence in U.S. schools, and the government's inability to stop it . . . is a big issue in school districts across the country."*

School Violence Threatens American Youth

Neal McCluskey

Despite efforts to reduce violence in America's schools, the problem continues, claims Neal McCluskey in the following viewpoint. School violence is underreported because standards for reporting vary—some schools report every punch; others fail to report felonious assaults, he maintains. Although the No Child Left Behind Act allows students from dangerous schools to transfer to those that are safe, vague definitions make it difficult to identify dangerous schools, McCluskey asserts. The only effective solution, he argues, is to allow parents to decide what schools are safe for their children. McCluskey is a policy analyst with Cato's Center for Educational Freedom.

As you read, consider the following questions:

1. What did writer Doug Oplinger discover when comparing police reports with reports filed by schools?

Neal McCluskey, "Violence in Public Schools: A Dirty Secret," *School Reform News*, June 1, 2005. Reproduced by permission.

2. What does McCluskey claim should be added to any list of recommendations to improve public school safety?

3. In the author's opinion, what is fueled by a lack of responsiveness to parents' concerns?

In March [2005], the public was startled by the news of a horrific shooting spree in Red Lake, Minnesota, where 16-year-old Jeff Wiese killed seven people and wounded at least 13 others at Red Lake High School before taking his own life—the deadliest school shooting since Columbine in 1999. [On Tuesday, April 20, 1999, at Columbine High School in Colorado, two students, Eric Harris and Dylan Klebold, killed 12 fellow students and a teacher before committing suicide.]

In mid-April [2005], the sexual assault of a 16-year-old special education student by a group of boys at a high school in Columbus, Ohio, which school officials tried desperately to keep under wraps for more than a month, made headlines across the country. The principal was fired and three assistant principals suspended without pay for failing to report the incident to police; one of the girl's assailants videotaped it.

Just a few weeks later, the parents of 19 Philadelphia elementary school students were shocked to learn their children had been stabbed by an eight-year-old classmate wielding a hypodermic needle and had to wait three hours before receiving medical attention. All had to be tested for HIV, and one student's preliminary results were positive.

Failing to Report Problems

These stories give parents, students, and policymakers cause for concern, and they are just a few examples of a broader school violence problem. Overall violence in U.S. schools, and the government's inability to stop it even when using new initiatives designed specifically for that purpose, is a big issue in school districts across the country.

According to the April 27 [2005] issue of *Education Week*, a February report by a Cleveland-based firm, National School

Safety and Security Services, found 86 percent of the 758 school officers surveyed said crimes at their schools were under-reported. Seventy-eight percent said they had personally taken weapons from students in the past year.

From reading the news, it would appear violence and danger are constant companions for America's schoolchildren. Though federal reports say school violence has been cut in half over the past decade, some analysts fear that could be because fewer administrators are willing to report the problem, not because violence is actually down.

"For the U.S. Department of Education to tell the American education community and public in general that school crime is declining is misleading," the firm's president, Kenneth S. Trump, told the magazine.

That assessment has been corroborated by several independent journalists around the country. For instance, in April [2005] the *Denver Post* examined massive under-reporting of violent incidents in Denver-area schools—under-reporting that occurred despite the presence of a state accountability system designed to identify dangerous schools. The problem in Colorado, and elsewhere, is that many schools simply do not report violent incidents.

A Growing Consensus

"In reality, disclosures of school violence vary wildly from one district to another. Some schools report every punch thrown on the playground. Others did not include assaults that police classified as felonies," *Denver Post* staff writer Doug Oplinger reported.

After comparing police reports with those filed by schools, Oplinger found serious discrepancies. Among the incidents that took place at metro-area schools reporting no violence or fights of any kind last year were a boy who needed staples to close head wounds; a girl who was hospitalized with bruised kidneys; a sexual assault; a knifing; and attacks with a flagpole and a baseball bat.

Between March and April [2005], the *Chicago Tribune* reported on the failure of law enforcement officials in Illinois to consistently notify school districts when convicted juvenile sex offenders enroll in their schools. Many failed to notify principals in the mistaken belief they were not permitted to alert them, when in fact they were required to do so.

In one case reported in the *Tribune*, an East Peoria school wasn't informed that a convicted 16-year-old sex offender had enrolled there until a seven-year-old victim's teenage brother told his mother that the assailant was in his gym class, and the mother told the school.

Fearing the Results

"I'm just one person in Peoria," the mother told the *Tribune*. "If [my son's assailant] fell through, how many other kids are out there that these schools don't know about?"

In *School Violence and No Child Left Behind: Best Practices to Keep Kids Safe*, a January 2005 report from the Reason Public Policy Institute (RPPI), education and child welfare director Lisa Snell examined school violence and the inadequacy of government systems to protect children. Her report focuses in particular on the No Child Left Behind Act (NCLB), which includes provisions enabling students to transfer from "persistently dangerous" public schools to those designated as "safe."

While in theory the idea is a good one, in practice it hasn't worked as intended, according to Snell's report. Few children have gotten the opportunity to leave dangerous schools because "evidence suggests that schools have unreasonable definitions of 'dangerous,' underreport school crime, and do not provide parents with accurate information about school crime," Snell wrote.

Watering Down the Data

When asked how the U.S. Department of Education is working to strengthen the "persistently dangerous" schools provisions of NCLB, Bill Modzeleski, associate assistant deputy secretary of the department's Safe and Drug-Free Schools Office, said one of the biggest hurdles NCLB faces is improving state and district data collection.

When the law was first passed in 2001, states often found some of their districts collected good data on school violence, while others did not. That, Modzeleski said, forced states to define "dangerous" using "lowest common denominator" data.

"Is that the best way of doing things? Probably not," he said. But he added that was the best that could be done with the available data. The department is currently working with states "to boost data collection systems," Modzeleski said.

In her report, Snell offered 10 recommendations for improving public school safety, including better data collection and reporting. Among those solutions, though, was one Modzeleski did not mention: eliminating state and federal restrictions on school choice.

School Choice Works

"Forced assignment to schools and the resulting mismatches and detachment beget boredom and violence and create schools that are unresponsive to parental demands for safer schools," Snell explained.

Echoing Snell's concerns, lack of responsiveness to parents' concerns is fueling a newer school danger: parental violence, like that by the Canton, Texas parent who shot his son's high school football coach this spring over the coach's handling of his son and the team.

In discussing the problem, Annette Lareau, a Temple University sociology professor, said in a March 20 [2005] *Philadelphia Inquirer* article, "sometimes, parents are extremely frustrated by what they see as the school's inability to protect their children and the school's lack of attention to the parents' concerns."

Although making NCLB's "persistently dangerous" provisions more rigorous might improve the situation, Snell said districts would still "be able to game it." The only cure, she said, is to let parents choose the schools their children attend and walk away from those that are dangerous.

"I think the right of exit is the only solution," she said.

> "Children are more than 100 times more likely to be murdered outside the school walls than within them."

School Violence Is a Decreasing Problem

Editors of the Economist

In the following viewpoint the editors of the Economist, *a British newsmagazine, maintain that violence in U.S. schools has declined. Fears of rising school violence stem from the extensive media coverage that often follows horrific but isolated incidents of violence, they claim. The media response leads to public overreaction to such events and a flurry of expert opinion on the causes of school violence, the authors argue. Unfortunately, the authors assert, Federal Bureau of Investigation (FBI) research following the 1999 Columbine massacre did not reveal a distinct profile of the school shooter.*

As you read, consider the following questions:

1. According to the *Economist*, to what did three fall 2006 school shootings lead?

2. By whom are most children murdered, in the authors' view?

3. In the authors' opinion, why is it difficult to extrapolate a culture of violence against women from a few, unusual examples?

To journalists, three of anything makes a trend. So after three school shootings in six days [during the fall of 2006], speculation about an epidemic of violence in American classrooms was inevitable, and wrong. Violence in schools has fallen by half since the mid-1990s; children are more than 100 times more likely to be murdered outside the school walls than within them.

Of course, that average is not wholly comforting. Most children who are murdered are murdered by someone they know. But most parents know with certainty that neither they nor their friends or relations are killers, so their worries focus on strangers. Their fears are inevitably stoked by the breathless coverage of school shootings.

Much to Mourn, Little to Learn

On September 27th [2006] a 53-year-old petty criminal, Duane Morrison, walked into a school in Bailey, Colorado, with two guns. He took six girls hostage, preferring the blondes, molested some of them, and killed one before committing suicide as police stormed the room.

On September 29th a boy brought two guns into his school in Cazenovia, Wisconsin. Prosecutors say that 15-year-old Eric Hainstock may have planned to kill several people. But staff acted quickly when they saw him with a shotgun, calling the police and putting the school into "lock-down." The head teacher, who confronted him in a corridor, was the only one killed.

And on October 2nd a 32-year-old milk-truck driver, Charles Roberts, entered a one-room Amish school in Nickel Mines, Pennsylvania. His suicide notes mentioned recurring dreams of molesting children, but it is unclear whether he did

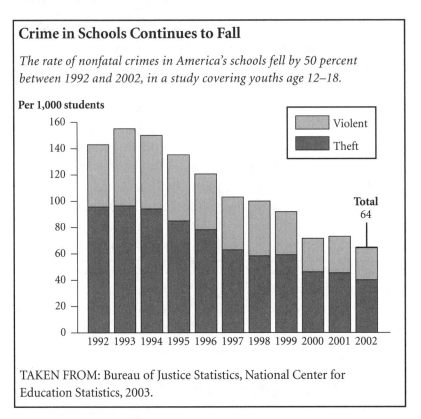

Crime in Schools Continues to Fall

The rate of nonfatal crimes in America's schools fell by 50 percent between 1992 and 2002, in a study covering youths age 12–18.

Per 1,000 students

TAKEN FROM: Bureau of Justice Statistics, National Center for Education Statistics, 2003.

so. He lined the girls up, tied their feet and, after an hour, shot them, killing at least five. He killed himself as police broke into the classroom.

No Easy Answers

What to make of such horrors? Some experts see the Colorado and Pennsylvania cases as an extreme manifestation of a culture of violence against women. Both killers appeared to have a sexual motive, and both let all the boys in the classroom go free. But it is hard to extrapolate from such unusual examples, and one must note that violence against women is less than half what it was in 1995.

Other experts see all three cases as symptomatic of a change in the way men commit suicide. Helen Smith, a forensic psychologist, told a radio audience "men are deciding to take their lives, and they're not going alone anymore. They're taking people down with them." True, but not very often.

Gun-control enthusiasts think school massacres show the need for tighter restrictions. It is too easy, they say, for criminals such as Mr Morrison and juveniles such as Mr Hainstock to obtain guns. Gun enthusiasts draw the opposite conclusion: that if more teachers carried concealed handguns, they could shoot potential child-killers before they kill.

[U.S. President] George [W.] Bush has now called for a conference on school violence. Will it unearth anything new or valuable? After the Columbine massacre in 1999 [in which two high school students killed twelve fellow students and a teacher before committing suicide] the FBI [Federal Bureau of Investigation] produced a report on school shooters. It concluded that it was impossible to draw up a useful profile of a potential shooter because "a great many adolescents who will never commit violent acts will show some of the behaviours" on any checklist of warning signs.

> "Domestic violence remains a pervasive threat to the fabric of America's families and the well-being of America's future."

Domestic Violence Is a Serious Problem

Dianne Feinstein

Domestic violence continues to pose a serious threat to American families, argues Senator Dianne Feinstein in the following viewpoint. Not only do American women continue to be victims of violence, but a significant number of teen girls have been hit or beaten by a dating partner, she maintains. Moreover, Feinstein claims, children who witness abuse or are themselves the victims of abuse often continue the cycle of violence. To stop this cycle, she asserts, continued attention to the problem of domestic violence as well as laws that protect its victims are necessary.

As you read, consider the following questions:

1. According to Senator Feinstein, how many incidents of domestic violence are reported each year?
2. How many children does the author claim witness domestic violence each year?

Dianne Feinstein, "Statement of Senator Dianne Feinstein: Domestic Violence in America," *Congressional Record*, vol. 150, no. 125, October 6, 2004.

3. What does Senator Feinstein claim the Victims' Rights Act will guarantee?

Today I rise with my colleague Senator [Jon] Kyl [R-Arizona] to commemorate Domestic Violence Awareness Month and to pay tribute to the millions of victims of domestic violence in the United States: both those who daily face fear and pain at the hands of the ones they love, and those who have had the courage to seek help.

A Pervasive Threat

Domestic violence causes far more pain than the visible marks of bruises and scars. It is devastating to be abused by someone that you love and think loves you in return. It is estimated that approximately 3 million incidents of domestic violence are reported each year in the United States. Tragically, domestic violence remains a pervasive threat to the fabric of America's families and the well-being of America's future.

Around the world, one out of three women is abused by their domestic partner or another member of their family. This means that each of us probably knows at least one victim of domestic abuse.

It is primarily a crime against women, who account for approximately eighty-five percent of domestic abuse victims each year. Indeed, nearly one-third of American women report being physically or sexually abused by a husband or boyfriend at some point in their lives, and each year as many as 324,000 women experience domestic violence during their pregnancy.

It is truly heartbreaking to hear these victims' stories and to know that so many women and even some men face this pain on a regular basis.

Domestic violence does not only happen to adults. Forty percent of girls age 14 to 17 report knowing someone their age who has been hit or beaten by a boyfriend, and approxi-

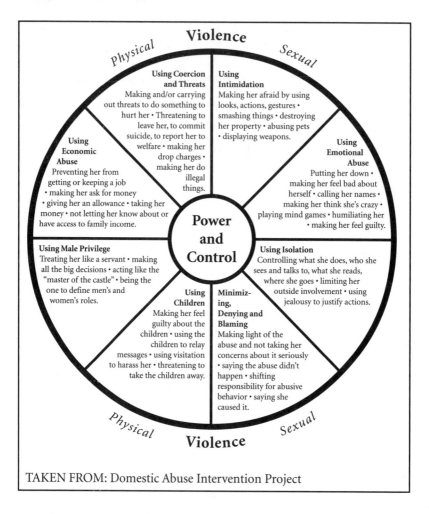

Violence

Physical · Sexual

Using Coercion and Threats
Making and/or carrying out threats to do something to hurt her · Threatening to leave her, to commit suicide, to report her to welfare · making her drop charges · making her do illegal things.

Using Intimidation
Making her afraid by using looks, actions, gestures · smashing things · destroying her property · abusing pets · displaying weapons.

Using Economic Abuse
Preventing her from getting or keeping a job · making her ask for money · giving her an allowance · taking her money · not letting her know about or have access to family income.

Using Emotional Abuse
Putting her down · making her feel bad about herself · calling her names · making her think she's crazy · playing mind games · humiliating her · making her feel guilty.

Power and Control

Using Male Privilege
Treating her like a servant · making all the big decisions · acting like the "master of the castle" · being the one to define men's and women's roles.

Using Isolation
Controlling what she does, who she sees and talks to, what she reads, where she goes · limiting her outside involvement · using jealousy to justify actions.

Using Children
Making her feel guilty about the children · using the children to relay messages · using visitation to harass her · threatening to take the children away.

Minimizing, Denying and Blaming
Making light of the abuse and not taking her concerns about it seriously · saying the abuse didn't happen · shifting responsibility for abusive behavior · saying she caused it.

Physical · Sexual

Violence

TAKEN FROM: Domestic Abuse Intervention Project

mately one in five female high school students reports being physically and/or sexually abused by a dating partner. And these are only the cases that are reported.

Additionally, many children are caught in the middle, witnessing abuse or being abused themselves. Domestic violence is witnessed by between 3.3 and 10 million children every year. And studies show that half of all men who frequently assault their wives also frequently abuse their children. The emotional impact of this abuse during childhood can have a devastating effect on the rest of a person's life.

A Cycle of Violence

Domestic abuse creates a cycle of violence. Children who are abused or witness abuse are at a higher risk of abusing their own family and significant others as an adult as well as long-term physical and mental health problems, including alcohol and substance abuse.

It is evident that these abuse victims follow the example they learned in childhood and continue the cycle of violence when they are adults.

Statistics can show us the wide scope of domestic violence, but numbers cannot demonstrate how frightening domestic violence is to a victim. I have read stories of many victims, both men and women, whose lives are changed forever by the fear and pain they feel as a result of their partner's violent behavior.

Shattered Stability

Let me talk about just one story I read recently. At first glance, Pam Butler appeared to have the perfect life. She grew up in a stable, loving family in Palo Alto, California. That stability was shattered when she met Michael Braga.

Michael Braga was a charismatic but troubled man who quickly romanced Pam Butler. He began to control every aspect of her life: limiting her contact with friends and family, controlling her money and living space and chipping away at her self-confidence. This behavior quickly escalated into violence.

Pam was beaten unconscious on several occasions. She painfully learned to hide the signs of the beatings because she was ashamed to be in such a horrible situation.

After several beatings caused re-injury to an old skull fracture, Pam Butler realized that staying in the relationship could kill her. She enlisted the help of Santa Clara County Assistant District Attorney Joyce Allegro.

I am pleased to report that Mr. Braga was arrested and prosecuted. Following his trial, he was sentenced to 12 years in prison, one of the longest sentences for domestic violence passed down in California history.

As a result of her experiences with domestic violence, Pam Butler has devoted many hours to assisting other victims. She is the Domestic Violence Victim Advocate for the County of Santa Clara's Social Services Agency. She has also spoken about domestic violence across the United States. Her story is an inspiration to every person who has been a victim of domestic violence.

Falling into the Same Trap

Another heartbreaking story is that of Michele, a Chicago woman who had been abused just as her mother and grandmother had before her. Michele's father hit and insulted her throughout her upbringing. Unfortunately, Michele was not able to break the cycle of violence and fell into the same trap as her mother and grandmother.

Her first husband beat her, cheated on her, called her insulting names and controlled her ability to come and go from her house. Although she was well-read and bright, Michele did not believe she had the ability to escape this horrible situation.

Ultimately, her husband left her and her children, and she continued the cycle of violence with other abusive men. Eventually, she and her children found themselves homeless. Only then did she realize that she could get help. Michele now encourages other victims to seek help and speak out against domestic violence.

Stopping the Cycle

It is vital that we act to stop the cycle of domestic violence. To this end, last April [2005] the Senate passed the Victims' Rights Act by a vote of 96 to 1. I am proud to have been a long-time supporter and co-sponsor of this important legislation. The Act amends the federal criminal code to expand the rights of victims, especially the protection of victims of domestic violence, during the course of an alleged offender's trial and imprisonment.

This is landmark legislation in its ability to ensure the rights of all victims, but it is especially important for victims of domestic abuse. The Victims' Rights Act assures victims the right to be reasonably protected from the accused. It guarantees the right to reasonable, accurate and timely notice of any public proceeding involving the crime, as well as any release or escape of the accused offender. And it protects the victim's right to be treated with fairness and with respect for his or her dignity and privacy.

The Victims' Rights Act is one of the most important pieces of legislation that I have had the privilege of supporting during my twelve years in the Senate. It is currently [as of 2004] before the House Subcommittee on Crime, Terrorism and Homeland Security, and I strongly encourage the House to take it up soon.

In closing, I am grateful for the opportunity to honor the victims of domestic violence and to call for an end to the cycle of violence. It is my sincere hope that we will all know peace and security in our own homes.

> *"If domestic violence were a major problem, one would expect those concerned . . . to resist [its] cheapening . . . whereby the stuff of lovers' quarrels becomes grounds for arrest."*

The Problem of Domestic Violence Is Exaggerated

Stephen Baskerville

Domestic violence is an exaggerated problem that threatens fathers' rights, claims Stephen Baskerville in the following viewpoint. Violent assault is already a crime, but one that requires due process protections, he maintains. When a matter is designated domestic violence, Baskerville asserts, however, constitutional protections are often circumvented. For example, he argues, restraining orders are issued without notice or a weighing of the evidence, thus criminalizing a father's contact with his own children. Baskerville is president of the American Coalition for Fathers and Children, a fathers' rights organization.

As you read, consider the following questions:

1. In Baskerville's view, how is today's political version of chivalry different from traditional chivalry?

2. According to the author, how does VAWA blur the distinction between violent crime and ordinary disagreements?

3. What type of violence are men much more likely to experience, in the author's opinion?

Feminists are playing the victim card with a vengeance, mostly because it is the only card left, with sympathy for feminism's strident campaigns at a low point. Yet beneath the media radar, victimhood has helped feminism advance virtually unopposed to aggrandize power in realms few perceive.

Victim politics requires exploiting traditional gender roles. This does not mean feminism has moderated, simply that it has exchanged ideological purity for power. Much as Stalinism [the political and economic system of the former, communist Soviet Union] inherited the habits of czarist absolutism and nationalism, feminism now exploits the stereotype of helpless damsels in distress and the public's good intentions.

Bureaucratic Gallantry

Today's foremost case in point is the Violence Against Women Act (VAWA), currently [as of 2005] up for reauthorization in Congress. VAWA appeals to mom-and-apple-pie sentiments: what legislator can oppose protecting women? The bill commands bipartisan sponsorship, and its renewal in 2000 was mostly unopposed.

Yet VAWA illustrates a serious problem with political conservatism and demonstrates how the Left advances despite its unpopularity. More than a failure of nerve, VAWA exemplifies a trend not so much to discard traditional values as to politicize them. Politicians can posture as champions of motherhood and family while turning them over to the safekeeping of the state. Thus domestic-violence legislation is pitched as an appeal to male chivalry, and Republicans are quick to volunteer. In contrast to traditional chivalry, however, today's political version does not proceed from personal duty and requires no risk or heroism. The gallantry feminists demand is bureaucratic, exercised by functionaries who wield state power that they expand as a result.

"Domestic violence" is now a vast and growing government industry. Yet the term has never been clearly defined. Given that criminal statutes against violent assault already exist, precisely what purpose is served by laws creating special categories of crime of which only some people can be victims? Domestic violence designates criminals politically, in terms of their membership in a group rather than acts they have actually committed. It also creates crimes based on relationships rather than deeds. Conflict that is not criminal between strangers becomes a crime between "intimate partners."

Circumventing Constitutional Protections

Whereas criminal assault charges require due process of law, designating a matter "domestic violence" circumvents constitutional protections. Law-abiding citizens are issued "restraining orders" that do not punish them for illegal actions but prohibit them from otherwise legal ones. Because violent assault is already punishable, the only people effectively restrained are peaceful ones.

Men's groups complain that VAWA excludes male victims and point to research showing that men are equally likely to be victims of domestic assault. Yet something more than "gender bias" is at work. Though advertised to protect women, VAWA's provisions are better seen as weapons in divorce and custody battles. As [family law attorney] Thomas Kasper writes in the *Illinois Bar Journal*, measures funded by VAWA readily "become part of the gamesmanship of divorce." Groups like the New Hampshire Coalition Against Domestic and Sexual Violence lobby strenuously on custody laws, using unverifiable assertions like "80% of fathers who desire shared custody of their children fit the profile of a batterer."

Restraining orders are routinely issued without any evidence of wrongdoing to criminalize fathers' contact with their own children. "Restraining orders and orders to vacate are granted to virtually all who apply," and "the facts have become irrelevant," writes Elaine Epstein, former president of the Massachusetts Women's Bar Association. "In virtually all cases, no notice, meaningful hearing, or impartial weighing of evidence is to be had."

Even feminists backhandedly acknowledge what the social-science literature clearly establishes: domestic violence and child abuse are overwhelmingly phenomena not of intact families but of separated and separating families and that the safest environment for women and children is a two-parent home. By encouraging marital breakup, VAWA exacerbates the problem it ostensibly exists to solve.

Blurring Distinctions

VAWA also blurs the distinction between violent crime and ordinary disagreement. Federally funded groups like the National Victim Assistance Academy (NVAA) and the Justice Department itself use vague and subjective terms to define "violence" where none took place: "extreme jealousy and possessiveness," "name-calling and constant criticizing, insulting, and belittling the victim," "blaming the victim for everything," "ignoring, dismissing, or ridiculing the victim's needs."

If domestic violence were a major problem, one would expect limited resources to be reserved for serious cases and those concerned about true violence to resist this cheapening of the language whereby the stuff of lovers' quarrels becomes grounds for arrest. Instead, activists use vague terms to imply criminal violence where none has taken place. In *The Battered Woman*, psychologist Lenore Walker excuses a woman who violently attacked her husband because he "had been battering her by ignoring her and by working late."

Concealing a Culture of Male Hatred

Far from being the leading cause of injury to women, domestic violence accounts for somewhat less than 2 percent of all women's injuries. . . .

National Electronic Injury Surveillance System data from 2000 . . . shows women's injuries from all types of violence amounts to 4.9 percent of the total. The leading cause of injury is falling down (28%), followed by vehicle accidents (18.1%).

The claim that domestic violence is the leading cause of injury is exaggerated by an order of magnitude, that is, by a factor of at least 10.

What cause is served by exaggerating the true incidences of domestic violence against women?. . .

Implicit in this domestic violence lie is a devastating indictment of men. Each of these grossly exaggerated number of women's domestic violence injuries must be mated with a male batterer.

Mark Charalambous, Mens News Daily,
November 11, 2004.

Though part of VAWA was declared unconstitutional on federalist grounds, the judiciary refuses to pass constitutional review. On the contrary, it is implemented by the very judiciary that is normally expected to protect constitutional rights. Strikingly, judges openly acknowledge the unconstitutionality—and their own indifference to it. "Your job is not to become concerned about all the constitutional rights of the man that you're violating as you grant a restraining order," New Jersey municipal court Judge Richard Russell told fellow judges at a government-run training seminar in 1994. "Throw him out on the street, give him the clothes on his back and tell him, 'See ya around.'"

Administering Feminist Justice

VAWA also funds special courts to administer not equal justice but feminist justice: ideological justice reminiscent of the French Revolution's political tribunals or [Adolf] Hitler's dreaded "people's courts." Some 300 "integrated domestic violence courts" now operate nationwide. In New York, Chief Judge Judith Kaye declares that the courts are created not to dispense impartial justice but to facilitate punishment: "to make batterers and abusers take responsibility for their actions."

These courts bear little relation to most Americans' understanding of due process. There is no presumption of innocence, hearsay evidence is admissible, and defendants have no right to confront their accusers. Even forced confessions are extracted. Warren County, Pennsylvania, requires fathers like Robert Pessia, on pain of incarceration, to sign prefabricated confessions stating, "I have physically and emotionally battered my partner." The father must then describe the violence, even if he insists he committed none. The formulaic documents state, "I am responsible for the violence I used. My behavior was not provoked."

VAWA Subsidizes Feminist Ideology

VAWA also subsidizes ideological advocacy of feminist organizations. Though Republicans in particular are feeding a mouth that bites them, the larger principle is whether taxpayers should ever sponsor political ideology. "If there is any fixed star in our constitutional constellation," wrote Supreme Court Justice Robert Jackson, "it is that no official, high or petty, can prescribe what shall be orthodox politics, nationalism, religion, or other matters of opinion."

Especially questionable is federal funding of lobbying by judges, who are professionally obligated to be apolitical. The National Council of Juvenile and Family Court Judges (NCJFCJ)—consisting of judges who sit on actual cases and are required to be impartial—receives federal support to attack fathers' groups and fathers themselves for being "at odds with the safety needs of the rest of the family." Can fathers summoned before these judges expect equal justice? NCJFCJ advocates administrative termination of paternal rights, termination of fathers' rights to see their children with no evidence of violence, ignoring officials who question abuse allegations, ignoring visitation orders, re-education of judges, and labeling law-abiding American citizens who criticize the government as "dangerous." They even seem to endorse the fabrication of evidence and a presumption of guilt. NVAA's Jacobin-style agenda [characterized by extremist or radical politics] is likewise endorsed and disseminated by the Justice Department: "establish a Family Violence Coordinating Council," "implement a massive community education program," "specialized domestic violence courts, and vertical prosecution," "fast track domestic violence prosecutions through priority docketing," "electronic monitoring," and "warrantless searches of their persons or homes."

Insidious Consequences

The complaint that VAWA excludes the large percentage of male victims is not petty. Men are much more likely to experience violence that is premeditated or contracted and which may be excluded from categorization as domestic violence: shootings in the back, hired killers, midnight castrations, attacks with cars. Not only does this violence seldom elicit public sympathy; it is not foremost among the terrors of men themselves. "The most common theme among abused men is their tales not of physical anguish but of dispossession," writes Patricia Pearson in *When She Was Bad*, "—losing custody of children due to accusations of physical and sexual abuse."

"They may never see their children again," says Philip Cook, author of *Abused Men*. "They don't feel that they will get a fair shake in the courts regarding custody no matter what happens or what she does. And it's actually true. There are many cases ... in which a woman who was actually arrested for domestic violence still receive[d] custody of the children." Losing custody is not the only danger: "A battered man knows that if his wife has been abusing him, she has often been abusing the children," writes [author and male rights advocate] Warren Farrell. "Leaving her means leaving his children unprotected from her abuse."

Here we arrive at the most insidious consequence of the moral grandstanding by VAWA's champions. Though advocates rhetorically intermingle child abuse with domestic violence, natural fathers commit a small fraction of child abuse; the overwhelming bulk is committed in single-parent homes. "Contrary to public perception," write Patrick Fagan and Dorothy Hanks of the Heritage Foundation, "the most likely physical abuser of a young child will be that child's mother, not a male in the household." Fathers commit 6.5 percent of child murders, according to a Justice Department study. The Department of Health and Human Services found that "women (the majority of whom are natural mothers) murder children 31.6 times more often than do natural fathers." A study by the Family Education Trust found children are up to 33 times more likely to be abused in a home without a father.

Erring on the Side of Danger

This is precisely the home environment VAWA subsidizes. Judges claim they remove fathers, even without evidence of abuse, to "err on the side of caution." In fact, they are erring on the side of danger, and it is difficult to believe they do not realize it. Recalling Dickens's observation that "the one great principle of the ... law is to make business for itself," the domestic-violence industry appears to be making business for itself by creating the environment conducive to child abuse.

Appalling as this sounds, this proceeds from the logic inherent in all bureaucracies: to perpetuate the problem they ostensibly exist to address. It gains plausibility from the verbal smoke-and-mirrors domestic-violence activists employ. "Adult domestic violence and child maltreatment often occur together," says Meredith Hofford of the NCJFCJ, "with the same assailant responsible for both." Hofford provides no documentation, but to the extent it is true, the "assailant" is likely to be not the father but the single mother. Hofford herself wants more money to "support" what she describes as "battered women who maltreat their children." This spiral of more funding to address the "needs" created by the previous funding illustrates how the domestic-violence juggernaut, and with it the crisis of family dissolution and fatherless children, will continue to expand until we learn to ignore hysterical people whom the government pays to cry wolf.

Periodical Bibliography

The following articles have been selected to supplement the diverse views presented in this chapter.

Thomas M. Achenbach   "Are American Children's Problems Still Getting Worse? A 23-Year Comparison," *Journal of Abnormal Child Psychology*, February 2003.

John M. Beam   "The Blackboard Jungle: Tamer than You Think," *New York Times*, January 20, 2004.

Pat Burson   "The Dark Side of Dating," *Los Angeles Times*, June 20, 2005.

Steve Chapman   "Juvenile Murders and Other Crimes," *Conservative Chronicle*, August 17, 2003.

Bob Herbert   "Why Aren't We Shocked?" *New York Times*, October 16, 2006.

Charles W. Huffine   "Youth Violence: Its Meanings to Society in the 21st Century," *Adolescent Psychiatry*, 2003.

Stephen Johnson and David B. Mulhausen   "North American Transnational Youth Gangs: Breaking the Chain of Violence," *Backgrounder* [Heritage Foundation], March 21, 2005.

Ira Leonard   "Violence Is the American Way," *AlterNet*, April 22, 2003.

Susannah Meadows   "Ghosts of Columbine," *Newsweek*, November 3, 2003.

Pamela M. Prah   "Domestic Violence," *CQ Researcher*, January 6, 2006.

Gretchen D. Werle   "Taking Steps to Promote Safer Schools," *Journal of School Health*, April 2006.

Cathy Young   "Oh Dad, Poor Dad: In Abuse, Men Are Victims, Too," *Boston Globe*, June 16, 2003.

Kate Zemike   "Violent Crime Rising Sharply in Some Cities," *New York Times*, February 12, 2006.

OPPOSING
VIEWPOINTS®
SERIES

CHAPTER 2

What Factors Contribute to Human Violence?

Chapter Preface

One of the most contentious debates in the United States concerns whether capital punishment should be accepted or abolished as a form of punishment. Commentators on both sides of the controversy offer several arguments to support their claims. One question that capital punishment analysts debate is whether capital punishment deters killing or instead actually contributes to human violence.

Those who support capital punishment claim that the practice reflects society's abhorrence of violence. Moreover, they assert that capital punishment acts as a deterrent to those who would kill others and in this way reduces violence. "Killing murderers," argues conservative radio talk-show host Dennis Prager, "is society's only way to teach how terrible murder is. The only real way a society can express its revulsion at any criminal behavior is through the punishment it metes out." Indeed, he maintains, "A society that kills murderers is saying that murder is more heinous a crime than a society that keeps all its murderers alive." Conservative commentator William Tucker agrees and adds that capital punishment also deters violence. "Since 1994," Tucker asserts, "states that have executed murderers have experienced the most rapid decline in homicide rates while states without capital punishment have seen an increase in murders." Three Emory University economists, Hashem Dezhbakhsh, Paul Rubin, and Joanna Shepherd, support Tucker's claim. These researches updated Isaac Ehrlich's 1976 analysis of capital punishment's deterrent effect. Ehrlich's report was presented as evidence before the 1976 Supreme Court when it reversed its moratorium on capital punishment. The Emory researchers concluded that "the execution of each offender seems to save, on average, the lives of 18 potential victims." Citing this evidence Tucker concludes that "capital punishment is a social policy that achieves targeted results."

Opponents argue that capital punishment does not teach that society is repulsed by murder and violence. In fact, argues political science professor and former judge Robert Grant, "Retributive justice . . . appeals to humanity's basest animal instincts and ancient demands for an eye for an eye, a life for a life. Retributive justice is fueled by hatred and satisfied only with full and complete revenge—the more cruel, the more satisfying." A peaceful society, opponents argue, resists the temptation for retribution and thus opposes capital punishment. "A more productive way to react to an act of violence," Grant maintains, "is to have the courage to resist the normal impulse for revenge and punishment, to refrain from allowing anger, hatred, rage, and vengeance to destroy one's inner peace." Capital punishment critics recommend restorative justice, the goal of which is to separate the violent person from a peaceful society. "Restorative justice," Grant reasons, "seeks to eliminate the culture of violence in U.S. society and replace it with a culture of caring." Grant acknowledges that "it's hard to put aside . . . feelings [of hatred] when a child or loved one is murdered, especially if the killing is particularly brutal or cruel." However, he reasons, "if we don't find a way to break the cycle of violence, we will never be able to end the culture of violence that infects the United States."

The capital punishment debate is one of the most enduring controversies in the United States. Whether it contributes to or deters violence in the United States is still hotly contested. The authors in the following chapter debate the impact of other factors believed to contribute to human violence.

| *"The spontaneous aggressiveness of humans is a harsh product of natural selection."* |

Human Violence Is a Product of Natural Selection

Richard Wrangham

Nature will select those humans who exploit weaknesses and kill their rivals, argues Richard Wrangham in the following viewpoint. Killing increases the aggressor's access to resources, he claims. Thus, killing is beneficial when competition for resources is fierce and killing poses little risk to the aggressor, Wrangham reasons. Violence among humans, however, is not inevitable, he claims. When power is balanced, the costs of violence outweigh the benefits, he concludes. Wrangham, a professor of biological anthropology at Harvard University, is author of Demonic Males: Apes and the Origins of Human Violence.

As you read, consider the following questions:

1. According to Wrangham, why are death rates from intergroup aggression among humans in nation-states lower than rates among hunter-gatherers?

2. In addition to humans and chimpanzees, what other mammal does the author claim has a significant inter-group killing rate?

3. In the author's opinion, what are the implications of human evolutionary ecology?

Warfare is often defined in a way that suggests it is unique to humans: for instance, as an interaction involving culturally sanctioned plans and weapons, or as organized fighting between large groups. But the behavior that underlies human warfare is not unique. Chimpanzees, our closest ape relatives, also have a tendency to organize into coalitions of related males to defend shared territory and to kill their enemies.

A Social Similarity

We are separated from chimpanzees by some 5 or 6 million years, and, more importantly, by enormous changes in ecology and ability, including differences in diet, locomotion, and sexuality, as well as by the refining influences of language and culture. Against this background, the significant social similarities are puzzling. Like humans, chimpanzees live in social communities with no fixed associations of individuals other than those between mothers and their dependent offspring. Accordingly, during the day, individuals can decide for themselves where to go. In hunter-gatherer societies most women forage in the company of other women, much as most male chimpanzees spend the day in the company of chosen allies. But in both cases, there are options. A woman might choose to make a tryst, stay in the camp, or walk alone. A male chimpanzee might equally well opt to travel alone for hours or days at a time. Such small and frequently changing subgroups within a community appear to be an important precondition for territorial aggression, which is one of the most striking similarities between humans and chimpanzees.

Most encounters between chimpanzee groups involve males. There can be as many as thirty-five males in a community, but the average is ten to twelve, and most temporary subgroups are about half that. Interactions with neighboring groups are never friendly and very often dangerous. Even so, males do sometimes seek out opportunities to engage their neighbors. Sometimes they climb a tree and face the neighboring range, listening for rivals. They routinely conduct border patrols and, tensed for an encounter, may venture beyond the zone of relative safety. Occasionally they make deep invasions.

Conflicts Among Chimpanzees

Most conflicts occur when parties surprise each other at close range—a few hundred yards, say. Calls from strangers prompt immediate tension. Sometimes the listeners briefly freeze, but more often they let out a volley of shouts and move quickly. If they are numerous, they advance. If not, they retreat toward the heart of their territory. But if the number of males on each side is similar, they usually stand their ground. Typically, chimpanzees in battle hurtle unpredictably through the brush, pausing tensely after each rush to look and listen, often standing bipedal with one hand on a small tree. These pauses allow them to gauge who's where, to find an ally, or to see uncertainty in the enemy. They then charge off on a new run across the battleground in groups of two or three. Occasionally one is hit by a passing rusher, but mostly the chimpanzees from each community charge back and forth from safe spots as each side tries to frighten the other into retreat. The air is thick with screams and emotion. It's hard to tell exactly what's happening in the melee of speed and power and fully erected hair. Their screams and barks can go on with hardly a pause for forty-five minutes.

In the end, the party with fewer males generally retreats, and tends to avoid the area for several weeks. The result can be significant, as this could mean the difference between eating from a rich fruit crop and being forced onto a poor diet that debilitates the adults and threatens infant survival.

When a lone combatant is caught by his rivals, the result tends to be remarkably lopsided. Several males each hold a hand or a foot of the captured rival, and the immobilized victim is damaged at will. Although the aggressors are unlikely even to be scratched, the victim may be killed on the spot, or bruised, bitten, and torn so badly that he survives only for a few days or weeks.

Death from Intergroup Aggression

The median death rate from intergroup aggression among chimpanzees is 140 per 100,000, which rises to 356 per 100,000 if suspected cases are included in addition to those observed or confidently inferred. Such death rates are similar to those resulting from war among humans in traditional subsistence societies, according to recent demographic data for thirty-two politically independent peoples, ranging from the relatively peaceful Semai of Malaysia to the famously dangerous Dani of New Guinea, among whom at least 28 percent of men's deaths, and 2 percent of women's, occurred in war. For hunter-gatherers, annual war deaths averaged 165 per 100,000, about the same as the minimum intergroup killing rate for chimpanzees. For subsistence farmers, the toll rose to a startling 595 per 100,000, somewhat above the upper estimate for chimpanzees.

Shockingly, death rates from intergroup aggression among humans in nation-states are lower, even when periods of major war are included. During the twentieth century, for example, Germany, Russia, and Japan each experienced rates of war deaths that were less than half the average hunter-gatherer rate. The contrast reflects a difference in the practice of war between pre-state and state societies. In pre-state societies, all men are warriors and all women are vulnerable. In state soci-

Violence Is Not Learned

If man is peaceful by nature, how is it that violence first entered his world? No one could have first learned it without someone to first teach it, but no one could first teach it without having first learned it. So it follows that, in the least, it certainly wasn't contrary to some people's nature.

The truth is that once you dispense with the tie-dyed tee-shirt, flowers-in-the-hair mentality and ponder how our ancestors stained battlefields red with ritualistic frequency, you realize one needn't be a cynic to believe that man doesn't have to be taught to be a barbarian.

He must be taught how not to be one.

Selwyn Duke, American Thinker, *April 6, 2007.*

eties, by contrast, fewer people are directly exposed to violence (even though civilians often suffer worse casualties than the military) because armies fight on behalf of the larger group.

The Killing Rate of Wolves

There's only one other mammal whose intergroup killing has been observed frequently enough to have been calculated: wolves, in the glacial uplands of Alaska's Denali National Park, an area free of human influences, 39 to 65 percent of adult wolves were killed by other packs. Similarly, in Minnesota, 43 percent of wolves not killed by humans were killed by other wolves.

Only the most extreme of human cultures match the killing rate of wolves. The highest human death rate from violence has been recorded among Waorani horticulturalists living in small dispersed villages in eastern Ecuador, where homicide takes the lives of 49 percent of women and 64 percent of men, close to the figure for Denali wolves.

Other pre-state societies show slightly lower figures, but the point is not to claim any particular numerical averages. It's merely to show that among chimpanzees, wolves, and humans the big picture is consistent: in typical populations of these three species, it can be mortally dangerous to meet the neighbors. That's why they all have war zones.

War Zones

War zones are the areas where territories abut, danger lurks, and parties rarely go. Low rates of foraging mean that war zones can become lands of plenty, rich in tempting resources. The Upper Missouri War Zone, a corridor 300 miles long and 150 miles wide, was a focal area for intertribal aggression among numerous indigenous groups, including the Nez Perce, Crow, and Shoshone. In 1805, [explorers Merriwether] Lewis and [William] Clark described the presence there of "immense quantities of buffalo in every direction"; the dangers of hunting in this area meant human predators avoided it, and it became a game sink. The Demilitarized Zone (DMZ) separating North and South Korea is so empty of people that it works the same way today, supporting large populations of rare and endangered species extinct on the rest of the Korean peninsula. Indeed, conservationists should be worried about the prospect of peace. When peace came to the Upper Missouri War Zone, many prey animals were hunted to extinction.

Population studies of chimpanzees' favorite prey species, red colobus monkeys, provide evidence of game sinks in chimpanzee war zones. Colobus group size is on average 46 percent smaller in the core of the territory than in border areas, where chimpanzees fear to go.

Wolf packs, too, keep clear of border areas except during periods of extreme food shortage. White-tailed deer therefore live at particularly high densities where wolf-pack territories overlap. The deer in these areas are critical for the long-term relationship between predator and prey, since they provide the stock for repopulating the overhunted areas near the centers of the wolf territories. Such war zones, in other words, provide conservation areas rather in the style of the Korean DMZ.

The abutment of territories alone, however, is not enough to make a war zone. Redtail monkeys in Kibale [National Park in Uganda] also live within defined territories, but they do not kill members of neighboring communities and they do not avoid territorial borders. They use their territories fully, right up to the border, and merely defend their ranges with chases when they meet encroaching neighbors. What makes a war zone is not a defined territory per se but the risk of being victimized at its edge.

An Evolutionary Explanation

In the great majority of species, territorial encounters involve display, chase, and occasional grappling, but not outright killing. There are only a select few species who avoid territorial boundaries for fear of death. The question is why this selection includes chimpanzees, wolves, and humans.

A strong evolutionary rationale for killing derives from the harsh logic of natural selection. Every homicide shifts the power balance in favor of the killers, giving them an increased chance of outnumbering their opponents and therefore of winning future territorial battles. Bigger territories also mean more food, and therefore more babies. This unpleasant formula implies that killing pays whenever resource competition is intense, and whenever killing can be carried out at low risk to the aggressors.

That humans in hunter-gatherer societies raided one another may seem surprising in view of the peaceful reputation of forager societies like the Kalahari Bushmen. There is, however, widespread evidence of violence among hunter-gatherers, even in the Kalahari: the shields of Eskimos attest to the occurrence of battles, and Australian Aborigines had weapons used exclusively for warfare, such as hooked boomerangs and heavy spears. Indeed, throughout the Arctic and in Australia, there is clear historical evidence of frequent raids and battles.

When Killing Is Cheap

The principle that underlies the mayhem is simple: When the killing is cheap, kill. In any particular instance it may or may not lead to a bigger territory, but from the perspective of natural selection, killing need only lead to benefits sufficiently often. Just as the first male fig wasp that emerges from pupation will immediately attempt to kill any other males he finds in the same fig, so humans, chimpanzees, and wolves benefit by killing rivals when it's reasonably safe to do so. The killers may think of their action as revenge, as a rite of manhood, of as placating the gods—or they may not think about it at all. They may do it simply because it's exciting, as seems to be the case for chimpanzees. The rationale doesn't matter to natural selection. What matters, it seems, is that in future battles the neighbors will have one less warrior.

For humans, chimpanzees, and wolves it makes sense to kill deliberately and frequently. Their protean grouping patterns mean they can choose to attack only when they have overwhelming power, which in turn means they can kill safely and cheaply, thereby winning a likely increase in resources over the succeeding months or years.

Evolutionary Ecology

Killing thus emerges as a consequence of having defined territories, dispersed groups, and unpredictable power relations. These conditions, in turn, appear to result from ecological adaptations, whether to a scattered fruit supply or to the challenges of hunting vertebrate prey. The implication is that because of our particular evolutionary ecology, natural selection has favored in the brains of humans, chimpanzees, and wolves a tendency to take advantage of opportunities to kill their rivals.

This doesn't condemn us to be violent in general. Indeed, within our communities humans are markedly less violent than most other primates, and in some ways humans are especially peaceful. Nor does it mean that intergroup aggression is inevitable; rather, it predicts little violence when power is balanced between neighboring communities. What it does imply, however, is that selection has favored a human tendency to identify enemies, draw moral divides, and exploit weaknesses pitilessly across boundaries.

Among hunter-gatherer societies, inner-city gangs, and volunteer militias at the fringes of contested national territories, there are similar patterns of violence. The spontaneous aggressiveness of humans is a harsh product of natural selection, part of an evolutionary morality that revels in short-term victory for one's own community without regard for the greater good.

| *"The crude picture of combat as the sole path to evolutionary success is wrong."*

Violence Is Not the Only Path to Evolutionary Success

Robert M. Sapolsky

Like many other primates, humans can be violent and aggressive, maintains Robert M. Sapolsky in the following viewpoint. However, he argues, aggression is not the primates' only route to evolutionary success. Bonobo chimpanzees and some troops of baboons have developed nonaggressive behaviors, Sapolsky asserts. Indeed, he claims, a few decades after World War II, Germany and Japan, once fierce aggressors, are now considered peaceful nations. Peaceful coexistence, he concludes, is not beyond human nature. Sapolsky, professor of biology and neurology at Stanford University, is author of Monkeyluv: And Other Essays on Our Lives as Animals.

As you read, consider the following questions:

1. In what way has human uniqueness been challenged most, in Sapolsky's view?

2. According to the author, why was the bonobo chimpanzee traditionally ignored by primatologists?

Robert M. Sapolsky, "A Natural History of Peace," *Foreign Affairs*, January–February 2006. Copyright © 2006 by the Council on Foreign Relations, Inc. All rights reserved. Reproduced by permission of the publisher, www.foreignaffairs.org.

3. In the author's opinion, what were the social consequences of the death of most male "Forrest Troop" savanna baboons to tuberculosis?

The evolutionary biologist Theodosius Dobzhansky once said, "All species are unique, but humans are uniquest." Humans have long taken pride in their specialness. But the study of other primates is rendering the concept of such human exceptionalism increasingly suspect.

Challenging Human Uniqueness

Some of the retrenchment has been relatively palatable, such as with the workings of our bodies. Thus we now know that a baboon heart can be transplanted into a human body and work for a few weeks, and human blood types are coded in Rh factors named after the rhesus monkeys that possess similar blood variability.

More discomfiting is the continuum that has been demonstrated in the realm of cognition. We now know, for example, that other species invent tools and use them with dexterity and local cultural variation. Other primates display "semanticity" (the use of symbols to refer to objects and actions) in their communication in ways that would impress any linguist. And experiments have shown other primates to possess a "theory of mind," that is, the ability to recognize that different individuals can have different thoughts and knowledge.

Our purported uniqueness has been challenged most, however, with regard to our social life. Like the occasional human hermit, there are a few primates that are typically asocial (such as the orangutan). Apart from those, however, it turns out that one cannot understand a primate in isolation from its social group. Across the 150 or so species of primates, the larger the average social group, the larger the cortex relative to the rest of the brain. The fanciest part of the primate brain, in other words, seems to have been sculpted by evolution to enable us to gossip and groom, cooperate and cheat, and obsess about who is mating with whom. Humans, in short, are yet another primate with an intense and rich social life—a fact that raises the question of whether primatology can teach us something about a rather important part of human sociality, war and peace.

Other Primates Kill Their Own

It used to be thought that humans were the only savagely violent primate. "We are the only species that kills its own," one might have heard intoned portentously at the end of nature films several decades ago. That view fell by the wayside in the 1960s as it became clear that some other primates kill their fellows aplenty. Males kill; females kill. Some kill one another's infants with cold-blooded stratagems worthy of Richard III [king of England whose reign is characterized by family infighting and murder]. Some use their toolmaking skills to fashion bigger and better cudgels. Some other primates even engage in what can only be called warfare—organized, proactive group violence directed at other populations.

As field studies of primates expanded, what became most striking was the variation in social practices across species. Yes, some primate species have lives filled with violence, frequent and varied. But life among others is filled with communitarianism, egalitarianism, and cooperative child rearing.

Patterns emerged. In less aggressive species, such as gibbons or marmosets, groups tend to live in lush rain forests where food is plentiful and life is easy. Females and males tend to be the same size, and the males lack secondary sexual markers such as long, sharp canines or garish coloring. Couples mate for life, and males help substantially with child care. In violent species, on the other hand, such as baboons and rhesus monkeys, the opposite conditions prevail.

The most disquieting fact about the violent species was the apparent inevitability of their behavior. Certain species seemed simply to be the way they were, fixed products of the interplay of evolution and ecology, and that was that. And although human males might not be inflexibly polygamous or come with bright red butts and six-inch canines designed for tooth-to-tooth combat, it was clear that our species had at least as much in common with the violent primates as with the gentle ones. "In their nature" thus became "in our nature." This was the humans-as-killer-apes theory popularized by the writer Robert Ardrey, according to which humans have as much chance of becoming intrinsically peaceful as they have of growing prehensile tails.

That view always had little more scientific rigor than a *Planet of the Apes* movie, but it took a great deal of field research to figure out just what should supplant it. After decades' more work, the picture has become quite interesting. Some primate species, it turns out, are indeed simply violent or peaceful, with their behavior driven by their social structures and ecological settings. More important, however, some primate species can make peace despite violent traits that seem built into their natures. The challenge now is to figure out under what conditions that can happen, and whether humans can manage the trick themselves.

Pax Bonobo

Primatology has long been dominated by studies of the chimpanzee, due in large part to the phenomenally influential research of Jane Goodall, whose findings from her decades of observations in the wild have been widely disseminated. *National Geographic* specials based on Goodall's work would always include the reminder that chimps are our closest relatives, a notion underlined by the fact that we share an astonishing 98 percent of our DNA with them. And Goodall and other chimp researchers have carefully documented an endless stream of murders, cannibalism, and organized group violence among their subjects. Humans' evolutionary fate thus seemed sealed, smeared by the excesses of these first cousins.

But all along there has been another chimp species, one traditionally ignored because of its small numbers; its habitat in remote, impenetrable rain forests; and the fact that its early chroniclers published in Japanese. These skinny little creatures were originally called "pygmy chimps" and were thought of as uninteresting, some sort of regressed subspecies of the real thing. Now known as bonobos, they are today recognized as a separate and distinct species that taxonomically and genetically is just as closely related to humans as the standard chimp. And boy, is this ever a different ape.

Male bonobos are not particularly aggressive and lack the massive musculature typical of species that engage in a lot of fighting (such as the standard chimp). Moreover, the bonobo social system is female dominated, food is often shared, and there are well-developed means for reconciling social tensions. . . .

Warriors, Come Out to Play

In contrast to the social life of bonobos, the social life of chimps is not pretty. Nor is that of rhesus monkeys, nor savanna baboons,—a species found in groups of 50 to 100 in the African grasslands and one I have studied for close to 30 years. Hierarchies among baboons are strict, as are their consequences. Among males, high rank is typically achieved by a series of successful violent challenges. Spoils, such as meat, are unevenly divided. Most males die of the consequences of violence, and roughly half of their aggression is directed at third parties (some high-ranking male in a bad mood takes it out on an innocent bystander, such as a female or a subordinate male). . . .

A baboon group, in short, is an unlikely breeding ground for pacifists. Nevertheless, there are some interesting exceptions. In recent years, for example, it has been recognized that a certain traditional style of chest-thumping evolutionary thinking is wrong. According to the standard logic, males compete with one another aggressively in order to achieve and maintain a high rank, which will in turn enable them to dominate reproduction and thus maximize the number of copies of their genes that are passed on to the next generation. But although aggression among baboons does indeed have something to do with attaining a high rank, it turns out to have virtually nothing to do with maintaining it. Dominant males rarely are particularly aggressive, and those that are typically are on their way out: the ones that need to use it are often about to lose it. Instead, maintaining dominance requires social intelligence and impulse control—the ability to form prudent coalitions, show some tolerance of subordinates, and ignore most provocations.

A Crude Model

Recent work, moreover, has demonstrated that females have something to say about which males get to pass on their genes. The traditional view was based on a "linear access" model of reproduction: if one female is in heat, the alpha male gets to mate with her; if two are in heat, the alpha male and the second-ranking male get their opportunity; and so on. Yet we now know that female baboons are pretty good at getting away from even champions of male-male competition if they want to and can sneak off instead with another male they actually desire. And who would that be? Typically, it is a male that has followed a different strategy of building affiliative relations with the female—grooming her a lot, helping to take care of her kids, not beating her up. These nice-guy males seem to pass on at least as many copies of their genes as their more aggressive peers, not least because they can go like this for years, without the life-shortening burnout and injuries of the gladiators.

And so the crude picture of combat as the sole path to evolutionary success is wrong. The average male baboon does opt for the combative route, but there are important phases of his life when aggression is less important than social intelligence and restraint, and there are evolutionarily fruitful alternative courses of action. . . .

Left Behind

In the early 1980s, "Forest Troop," a group of savanna baboons I had been studying—virtually living with—for years, was going about its business in a national park in Kenya when a neighboring baboon group had a stroke of luck: its territory encompassed a tourist lodge that expanded its operations and consequently the amount of food tossed into its garbage dump. Baboons are omnivorous, and "Garbage Dump Troop" was delighted to feast on leftover drumsticks, half-eaten hamburgers, remnants of chocolate cake, and anything else that wound up there. Soon they had shifted to sleeping in the trees immediately above the pit, descending each morning just in time for the day's dumping of garbage. (They soon got quite obese from the rich diet and lack of exercise, but that is another story.)

The development produced nearly as dramatic a shift in the social behavior of Forest Troop. Each morning, approximately half of its adult males would infiltrate Garbage Dump Troop's territory, descending on the pit in time for the day's dumping and battling the resident males for access to the garbage. The Forest Troop males that did this shared two traits: they were particularly combative (which was necessary to get the food away from the other baboons), and they were not very interested in socializing (the raids took place early in the morning, during the hours when the bulk of a savanna baboon's daily communal grooming occurs).

Soon afterward, tuberculosis, a disease that moves with devastating speed and severity in nonhuman primates, broke

Human Violence Is Not Instinctive

War is too complex and collective an activity to be accounted for by any warlike instinct lurking within the individual psyche. Battles, in which the violence occurs, are only one part of war, most of which consists of preparation for battle—training, the manufacture of weapons, the organization of supply lines, etc. There is no plausible instinct, for example, that could impel a man to leave home, cut his hair short, and drill for hours in tight formation.

Barbara Ehrenreich, "The Roots of War," Progressive, April 2003.

out in Garbage Dump Troop. Over the next year, most of its members died, as did all of the males from Forest Troop who had foraged at the dump. The results were that Forest Troop was left with males who were less aggressive and more social than average and the troop now had double its previous female-to-male ratio.

The Social Consequences

The social consequences of these changes were dramatic. There remained a hierarchy among the Forest Troop males, but it was far looser than before: compared with other, more typical savanna baboon groups, high-ranking males rarely harassed subordinates and occasionally even relinquished contested resources to them. Aggression was less frequent, particularly against third parties. And rates of affiliative behaviors, such as males and females grooming each other or sitting together, soared. There were even instances, now and then, of adult males grooming each other—a behavior nearly as unprecedented as baboons sprouting wings.

This unique social milieu did not arise merely as a function of the skewed sex ratio; other primatologists have occasionally reported on troops with similar ratios but without a comparable social atmosphere. What was key was not just the predominance of females, but the type of male that remained. The demographic disaster—what evolutionary biologists term a "selective bottleneck"—had produced a savanna baboon troop quite different from what most experts would have anticipated.

But the largest surprise did not come until some years later. Female savanna baboons spend their lives in the troop into which they are born, whereas males leave their birth troop around puberty; a troop's adult males have thus all grown up elsewhere and immigrated as adolescents. By the early 1990s, none of the original low aggression/high affiliation males of Forest Troop's tuberculosis period was still alive; all of the group's adult males had joined after the epidemic. Despite this, the troop's unique social milieu persisted—as it does to this day, some 20 years after the selective bottleneck. In other words, adolescent males that enter Forest Troop after having grown up elsewhere wind up adopting the unique behavioral style of the resident males. As defined by both anthropologists and animal behaviorists, "culture" consists of local behavioral variations, occurring for nongenetic and nonecological reasons, that last beyond the time of their originators. Forest Troop's low aggression/high affiliation society constitutes nothing less than a multigenerational benign culture. . . .

Culture Simply Emerges

At present, I think the most plausible explanation is that this troop's special culture is not passed on actively but simply emerges, facilitated by the actions of the resident members. Living in a group with half the typical number of males, and with the males being nice guys to boot, Forest Troop's females become more relaxed and less wary. As a result, they are more willing to take a chance and reach out socially to new arrivals, even if the new guys are typical jerky adolescents at first. The new males, in turn, finding themselves treated so well, eventually relax and adopt the behaviors of the troop's distinctive social milieu.

Natural Born Killers?

Are there any lessons to be learned here that can be applied to human-on-human violence—apart, that is, from the possible desirability of giving fatal cases of tuberculosis to aggressive people? . . .

In the early 1960s, a rising star of primatology, Irven De-Vore, of Harvard University, published the first general overview of the subject. Discussing his own specialty, savanna baboons, he wrote that they "have acquired an aggressive temperament as a defense against predators, and aggressiveness cannot be turned on and off like a faucet. It is an integral part of the monkeys' personalities, so deeply rooted that it makes them potential aggressors in every situation." Thus the savanna baboon became, literally, a textbook example of life in an aggressive, highly stratified, male-dominated society. Yet within a few years, members of the species demonstrated enough behavioral plasticity to transform a society of theirs into a baboon utopia.

The first half of the twentieth century was drenched in the blood spilled by German and Japanese aggression, yet only a few decades later it is hard to think of two countries more pacific. Sweden spent the seventeenth century rampaging through Europe, yet it is now an icon of nurturing tranquility. Humans have invented the small nomadic band and the continental megastate, and have demonstrated a flexibility whereby uprooted descendants of the former can function effectively in the latter. We lack the type of physiology or anatomy that in other mammals determine their mating system, and have come up with societies based on monogamy, polygyny, and polyandry. And we have fashioned some religions in which violent acts are the entrée to paradise and other religions in which the same acts consign one to hell. Is a world of peacefully coexisting human Forest Troops possible? Anyone who says, "No, it is beyond our nature," knows too little about primates, including ourselves.

> *"The proportion of blacks and Hispanics in an area is the single best indicator of how dangerous it is."*

Blacks and Hispanics Are More Likely to Commit Violent Crimes

Jared Taylor

Federal crime database statistics reveal that blacks and Hispanics are more likely to commit violent crimes than whites, argues Jared Taylor in the following viewpoint. Moreover, he claims, whites are more likely to be the victims. The mainstream media refuse to report these statistics, fearing the racist label, Taylor maintains. By failing to report that people of color commit a majority of crimes in the United States, the media are suggesting that Americans cannot be trusted with the truth, he asserts. Taylor is editor of American Renaissance, *a magazine that openly examines racial differences.*

As you read, consider the following questions:

1. According to Taylor, how many more times is a black likely to do violence to a white than vice versa?

Jared Taylor, "Color of Crime, Sound of (Big Media) Silence," *Vdare.com*, September 13, 2005. Copyright © 1999–2007 VDARE.com. Reproduced by permission.

2. Why did Frank Jewell, head of Violence Free Duluth, not reveal the race of the perpetrator in its crime study, in the author's view?

3. In the author's opinion, why do people go to the Internet for facts?

For anyone who ever wondered just how much more likely blacks or Hispanics are than whites to commit various crimes, the answers are here.

Looking at the Statistics

It takes hard work to pry the facts out of the reluctant grip of federal crime databases. But the results are eye-opening:

- Blacks are just 13 percent of the population but they commit more than half the muggings and murders in the country. Hispanics commit violent crimes at about three times the white rate.

- The proportion of blacks and Hispanics in an area is the single best indicator of how dangerous it is. The racial mix is a much better predictor of crime rates than poverty, unemployment, and dropout rates combined.

- Although [black civil rights activist and minister] Jesse Jackson and [black entertainer and activist] Bill Cosby wring their hands over black-on-black mayhem, blacks actually commit more violent crime against whites than blacks. A black is about 39 times more likely to do violence to a white than the other way around, and no less than 130 times more likely to rob a white.

- And yes, everyone's suspicions about rape are correct: Every year there are about 15,000 black-on-white rapes but fewer than 900 white-on-black rapes. There are more than 3,000 gang rapes of whites by blacks—but white-on-black gang rapes are so rare they do not even show up in the statistics.

There is plenty more—but just as interesting will be how the Mainstream Media will treat these facts.

Media Silence

Back in 1999, we released an earlier, less detailed version of this report. Even before publication, the Associated Press [AP], *Time, CBS Evening News*, National Public Radio, Knight-Ridder, and the *Washington Times* wanted copies. A dozen other media organizations, including the *Washington Post*, attended the press conference with which we launched the report. At the same time, we arranged to have copies delivered to more than 450 news organizations with offices in the Washington, DC area.

The result: complete silence—with one exception. The *Washington Times* ran a substantial story on the report, in which it interviewed several prominent criminologists who confirmed the accuracy of our numbers but said they were too inflammatory to be discussed publicly.

Maybe no other editors thought people are interested in race and crime.

Or maybe they were afraid people are *too* interested.

Some years back, a group called Violence Free Duluth in Duluth, Minnesota, studied a year's worth of the city's gun crimes. They looked into type of gun used, whether liquor or drugs were involved, the relationship between shooter and victim; age, race, and sex of criminal, etc.

But when they released their report they left one thing out: race of perp[etrator].

Frank Jewell, head of the organization, explained that "we didn't include it because it might be misinterpreted."

Unreported Victims

The most likely victim of a hate crime in the U.S. is a poor, young, white, single urban dweller, according to an analysis of Justice Department statistics collected from between July 2000 and December 2003.

A November [2005] report by the Bureau of Justice Statistics detailing a study of 210,000 "hate crimes" a year during that period has gone virtually unreported by the U.S. press.

Joseph Farah, World NetDaily.com, 2006.

Race May Detract from Real Problem

Duluth's deputy police chief Robert Grytdahl added that race might distract whites from the real problem: "It's a comfortable place for white people to park the [gun crime] problem. It would be a huge distraction, and we wanted to focus on firearms."

Mr. Jewell and Mr. Grytdahl are saying, almost in so many words, that the people of Duluth can't be trusted with the truth.

Duluth is about 90 percent white. What if it turned out most of the gun crime was committed by the other 10 percent?

Someone might think Duluth has, not a gun problem, but a minority problem.

When an organization deliberately suppresses its findings like this, it is not doing research: it is putting out propaganda.

It is impossible to know whether the national media suppressed the findings in our earlier report or just didn't think they were newsworthy. But if they thought no one was interested in race and crime they were wrong. Radio talk show hosts greeted the report with shouts of joy.

Over the years, I have spoken on hundreds of radio programs. But no other subject has ever caught the attention of hosts and listeners the way this one did.

Over and over, I was asked to stay on the program longer than scheduled because listeners could not get enough. Producers called up a week later and had me back again because listeners demanded it. Some producers even called because they had heard me on a rival station and wanted a piece of the ratings bonanza.

Trusting Whites with the Truth

Most whites lose the power of speech when the subject is race, but they can tuck right into a purely factual discussion of crime rates. Everybody—and I mean *everybody*—knows blacks commit crime way out of proportion to their numbers. People want to know just how way out the proportions are.

Needless to say, some listeners didn't want to hear that blacks are in jail for robbery at 15 times the white rate. A surprising number of black callers claimed our "racist" white government cooks the statistics. Most white callers said one of two things: either that I was "racist" or that I was brave. (Somehow, no one ever thought I was a brave racist.)

It is a sorry day in America when you are either brave or racist if you dig up and publicize crime data the Department of Justice has been collecting for decades.

The main point of the "racism" accusation was that, even if the numbers were true, publicizing them only encourages other "racists" and feeds stereotypes. This is the Frank Jewell argument: White people can't be trusted with the facts.

Of course, the Internet makes it hard to keep facts under the rug. People know the big media are full of pablum; that's why they come to sites like VDARE.COM and my own *American Renaissance*.

In fact, more and more people are laughing outright at mainstream prudery. When I talked about crime on the radio, talk-show hosts were exultant: "You didn't read about this in the *Baltimore Sun* did you? That's right, folks, this is where you get the real news."

This time around, it would be pleasant if AP or the *LA Times* wrote about *The Color of Crime*.

But we're not counting on it.

The Internet and talk radio will get the word out—and big media will sink just a little further in the minds of people who are tired of being told they can't be trusted with the truth.

> *"When community and personal economic status is comparable between whites and blacks, there are no significant racial crime differences."*

Higher Minority Crime Rates Do Not Justify White Fear or Racial Profiling

Tim Wise

The facts do not support the claim that blacks commit more crimes than whites, asserts Tim Wise in the following viewpoint. Studies show no crime-rate differences when economic conditions among whites and blacks are the same, he maintains. The purpose of such claims is to stoke fears that blacks are targeting whites, Wise argues. Such claims are spurious, he reasons, since blacks are significantly less likely to encounter whites, and crime statistics show that blacks victimize whites less often than probability would suggest. Wise, an antiracist activist, is author of White Like Me: Reflections on Race from a Privileged Son.

As you read, consider the following questions:

1. In what sorts of destructive behaviors does Wise claim whites lead the way?

Tim Wise, "The Color of Deception," *ZNet, www.zmag.org*, November 19, 2004. Reproduced by permission.

2. What percentage of Latinos are considered racially white by government record keepers, in the author's view?

3. If crime data can justify white fear of blacks, whom does Wise argue it should also require whites to fear?

"A lie can travel half-way around the world while the truth is still pulling on its boots."

Although this truism was penned long before the Internet, there is little doubt but that in the modern era, it has become more prescient than its author could ever have imagined.

When it comes to fast-moving lies, few can top one that has been distributed by white supremacists for the past several years. It is probably the most popular piece of racist propaganda in existence today, and because it relies on official government data, it comes across as sober, intelligent social science, rather than as the compendium of nonsense it happens to be.

The screed to which I refer is *The Color of Crime: Race, Crime and Violence in America*, by white nationalist, Jared Taylor. Taylor is the publisher of the racist magazine, *American Renaissance*, and host of an annual conference, which attracts open neo-Nazis as well as a gaggle of academicians who proclaim black genetic inferiority. According to Taylor, there are several "facts" about crime that have been hidden from view by the civil rights community. Among them:

- Blacks are much more dangerous than whites as evidenced by higher crime rates;

- Black criminals usually choose white victims and are far more likely to victimize whites than whites are to victimize blacks (both for regular violent crimes and hate crimes);

- Black crime rates justify racial profiling, since it only makes sense to focus law enforcement attention on those who commit a disproportionate share of crime; and finally,

- The interracial crime data makes white fear of African Americans perfectly rational.

But a close examination of these arguments proves that Taylor and his followers are either statistically illiterate, or knowingly deceive for political effect.

First, as for the disproportionate rate of violent crime committed by blacks, economic conditions explain the difference with white crime rates. According to several studies, when community and personal economic status is comparable between whites and blacks, there are no significant racial crime differences. In other words, the implicit message of Taylor's report—that blacks are dangerous because they are black—is insupportable.

Secondly, to claim that blacks are more dangerous than whites because of official crime rates, is to ignore that when it comes to everyday threats to personal well-being, whites far and away lead the pack in all kinds of destructive behaviors: corporate pollution, consumer fraud, violations of health and safety standards on the job, and launching wars on the basis of deceptive evidence, to name a few. Each year, far more people die because of corporate malfeasance, occupational health violations and pollution than all the street crime combined, let alone street crime committed by African Americans.

Stoking Fears About Interracial Crime— A Look at How Racists Do Math

Next, Taylor claims that most victims of black violent crime are white, and thus, that blacks are violently targeting whites. Furthermore, since only a small share of the victims of white criminals are black (only 4.4 percent in 2002, for example), this means that blacks are far more of a threat to whites than vice-versa. But there are several problems with these claims.

To begin with, the white victim totals in the Justice Department's victimization data include those termed Hispanic by the Census, since nine in ten Latino/as are considered racially white by government record-keepers. Since Latinos and Latinas tend to live closer to blacks than non-Hispanic whites, this means that many "white" victims of "black crime" are Latino or Latina, and that in any given year, the majority of black crime victims would be people of color, not whites.

Taylor's Position Is Without Merit

But even if we compute the white totals as Taylor does, without breaking out Hispanic victims of "black crime," his position is without merit. In 2002, whites, including Latinos, were about 81.5 percent of the population. That same year, whites (including Latinos) were 51 percent of the victims of violent crimes committed by blacks, meaning that whites were victimized by blacks less often than would have been expected by random chance, given the extent to which whites were available to be victimized.

As for the claim that blacks victimize whites at rates that are far higher than the reverse, though true, this statistic is meaningless, for a few obvious but overlooked reasons, first among them the simple truth that if whites are more available as potential victims, we would naturally expect black criminals to victimize whites more often than white criminals would victimize blacks. Examining data from 2002, there were indeed 4.5 times more black-on-white violent crimes than the reverse. While this may seem to support Taylor's position, it actually destroys it, because the interracial crime gap, though seemingly large, is smaller than random chance would have predicted. The critical factor ignored by Taylor is the extent to which whites and blacks encounter each other in the first place. Because of ongoing racial isolation and de facto segregation, the two groups' members do not encounter one another at rates commensurate with their shares of the population: a fact that literally torpedoes the claims in *The Color of Crime.*

As sociologist Robert O'Brian has noted (using Census data), the odds of a given white person (or white criminal for that matter) encountering a black person are only about three percent. On the other hand, the odds of a given black person (or black criminal) encountering a white person are nineteen times greater, or fifty-seven percent, meaning the actual interracial victimization gap between black-on-white and white-on-black crime is smaller than one would expect. In 2002, blacks committed a little more than 1.2 million violent crimes, while whites committed a little more than three million violent crimes. If each black criminal had a 57 percent chance of encountering (and thus potentially victimizing) a white person, this means that over the course of 2002, blacks should have been expected to victimize roughly 690,000 whites. But in truth, blacks victimized whites only 614,176 times that year. Conversely, if each white criminal had only a three percent chance of encountering and thus victimizing a black person, this means that over the course of 2002, whites would have been expected to victimize roughly 93,000 blacks. But in truth, whites victimized blacks 135,931 times: almost 50 percent more often than would be expected by random chance.

Indeed, given relative crime rates as well as rates of interracial encounter, random chance would have predicted the ratio of black-on-white to white-on-black victimization at roughly 7.4 to one. Yet, as the data makes clear, there were only 4.5 times more black-on-white crimes than white-on-black crimes in 2002. In other words, given encounter ratios, black criminals victimize whites less often than could be expected, while white criminals victimize blacks more often than could be expected.

Lies About Hate Crimes—More Fun with Racist Math

Taylor's claims regarding hate crimes are even more ridiculous. So, for example, *The Color of Crime* asserts that blacks commit a disproportionate share of racial and ethnic hate crimes against whites, while white-on-black hate crimes are far less frequent. But the data simply doesn't support such a claim.

From 1995–2000, blacks were 65 percent of racial and ethnic hate-crime victims, while whites were 21 percent of such victims. Adjusted for population, any given black person was nearly twenty times more likely to be the victim of a racially motivated hate crime than any given white. In 2001, there were approximately 4.6 times more white-on-black than black-on-white hate crimes, despite the fact that whites were between six and seven times more available in the population to become victims. Considering that blacks are much more likely to encounter whites than vice-versa, this last statistic is especially alarming. After all, if blacks are nineteen times more likely to encounter whites than whites are to encounter blacks, any given black person would have nineteen times more opportunities to commit an anti-white hate crime than a white person would have to commit an anti-black hate crime.

Differential Rates of Encounter

Since blacks are roughly one-sixth the size of the non-Hispanic white population, in order to determine the expected ratio of black-on-white hate crimes relative to white-on-black hate crimes given random chance, one must multiply the 19:1 black-on-white encounter ratio by one-sixth. Once this computation is made, we find that differential rates of encounter and population availability would predict that if levels of racial hatred were equal between whites and blacks, and the willingness to commit a hate crime were equal between the two groups, in any given year there should be 3.15 times more black-on-white hate crimes than white-on-black hate crimes. That in truth there are nearly five times more white-on-black hate crimes than the reverse suggests that blacks are much less likely to commit an anti-white hate crime than would be expected and whites are far more likely to commit an anti-black hate crime than would be expected.

White Fear of Blacks—The Height of Irrationality

Of course, above and beyond the mere statistical chicanery at the heart of Taylor's report, the larger point is that for Taylor and other racists to claim that black-on-white crime data justifies white fear of African Americans, or racial profiling by police is sheer ignorance.

Criminologists estimate that seventy percent of all crimes are committed by just seven percent of the offenders: a small bunch of repeat offenders who commit the vast majority of crimes. Since blacks committed roughly 1.2 million violent crimes in 2002, if seventy percent of these were committed by seven percent of the black offenders, this would mean that at most there were perhaps 390,000 individual black offenders that year. In a population of 29.3 million over the age of twelve, this would represent no more than 1.3 percent of the black population that committed a violent crime in 2002. Since fewer than half of these would have chosen a non-Hispanic white victim (as noted previously), this means that less than seven-tenths of one percent of the black population would have victimized a white person in 2002: hardly the kind of fact that would warrant white fear of blacks as a group.

Furthermore, since whites were victimized 2.9 million times by other whites in 2002 (compared to roughly 614,000 times by blacks), this means that whites are 4.7 times more likely to be victimized by another white person than by a black person. Thus, if crime data can justify white fear of blacks, it would also require whites to be terrified of white neighbors, co-workers, family and white strangers, for these are the folks most likely to victimize us.

The Absurdity of Profiling

As for profiling, Taylor insists that because of higher black crime rates, it only makes good sense to focus police efforts on the black community. But this is demonstrably ludicrous.

If, as the Justice Department data suggests, blacks commit somewhere between 25–30 percent of violent crime in most years (23 percent in 2002), to profile blacks for crime will result in police being wrong, between 70–75 percent of the time. And of course, profiling is not the typical method for uncovering serious already-committed crimes anyway, since solving such crimes logically involves using incident-specific information. Profiling is, instead, too often done as a way to uncover crimes, such as drug possession, that have yet to come to police attention.

As for drugs, there can be no doubt that profiling is irrational. According to federal data, blacks are only 13.5 percent of drug users, while non-Hispanic whites are over 70 percent of users. So to profile blacks for drugs is to guarantee little success in actually uncovering drug crimes.

Why Bother Responding to Professional Racists?

Some may wonder whether it makes sense to spend so much time and energy responding to the claims of someone who openly consorts with neo-Nazis, and whose agenda is so blatantly racist in nature. Though it would be nice not to have to respond to such silliness, the fact is, Taylor and his report have been cited approvingly by conservative columnists and talking heads, from [conservative columnist] Walter Williams, to [conservative writer and activist] David Horowitz, to the folks at the *National Review*, to Vanderbilt Law professor, Carol Swain.

What's more, with studies suggesting that white perceptions of black criminality play a prominent role in furthering racism, both attitudinally and institutionally (in terms of support for racially disparate and draconian crime policies), refuting this kind of foolishness carries with it important personal and policy implications as well.

However unappealing it may be to have to answer the racist claims of bigots and fascists, the fact remains that given the appeal of racist logic to so many, and given the strength of institutional racism as a defining force in American life, we can hardly afford the luxury of ignoring such positions, so as to "not give them legitimacy." The sad fact is that racism already enjoys plenty of legitimacy, with or without a rebuttal. Ignoring this reality isn't likely to diminish its strength, but responding to it forcefully might, at the very least, dissuade impressionable minds from accepting the twisted logic offered by the racist right.

"Experts in all camps would likely agree that domestic violence is a complex problem affected by multiple variables."

The Causes of Domestic Violence Are Complex

Diana Mahoney

Because the root causes of domestic violence are complex, it continues to be a serious problem, claims Diana Mahoney in the following viewpoint. While some theorists contend that the underlying cause of domestic violence is biological, others believe the cause is psychopathological, shaped by early childhood experiences, she asserts. Still others believe that domestic violence is learned within dysfunctional families, and some claim inequitable social views of women is the cause. All theories suggest that prevention efforts aimed toward at-risk children offer the best hope of reducing domestic violence. Mahoney writes for Clinical Psychiatry News, *a monthly newsmagazine for practitioners.*

As you read, consider the following questions:

1. According to Mahoney, why are domestic violence interventions not enough?

2. To what does the author compare trying to stop domestic violence without getting to its root?

3. In the author's opinion, what are some of the higher-risk populations for domestic violence?

Most interventions for domestic violence are, by design, crisis oriented. They seek to curtail the cycle of violence by identifying, protecting, and perhaps strengthening people who have already been injured, by attempting to rehabilitate perpetrators, or by promoting community awareness of the problem.

Such interventions are effective—to a degree. According to national statistics, domestic violence-related homicides have decreased significantly over the last 20 years [between 1985 and 2005], presumably in part because of increased public awareness and the growing number of resources available to help victims. But these interventions do not prevent the damage from occurring in the first place, because they often fail to go deep enough into the gnarled root system to address the core causes.

Looking at the Numbers

According to the CDC's [Centers for Disease Control and Prevention's] National Center for Injury Prevention and Control, domestic violence incidents cause nearly 2 million injuries and 1,300 deaths each year. "Across the country, more than three women are murdered by their husbands or boyfriends every day. One in every three women will be physically assaulted by a partner, and every year, 10 million children experience domestic violence in their homes," said Judith Kahan, chief executive officer of the Center Against Domestic Violence in Brooklyn, N.Y. "In New York City, if you added up all the reported robberies, burglaries, and murders in 2003 and multiplied that number by 2, it still would not equal the number of calls received by the city's domestic violence hot line."

What Are the Causes of Domestic Abuse or Domestic Violence?

An individual who was abused as a child or exposed to domestic violence in the household while growing up is at an increased risk of becoming either an abuser or the abused in his or her adult relationships. In this way, domestic violence and abuse is transmitted from one generation to the next. This cycle of domestic violence is difficult to break because parents have presented abuse as the norm.

Other factors that can lead to domestic abuse include:

- Stress

- Economic hardship

- Depression

- Jealousy

- Mental illness

- Substance abuse

Tina de Benedicts, Jaelline Jaffee, and Jeanne Segal,
HelpGuide.org, 2007.

In addition to the physical, emotional, and social costs of such abuse, the financial costs are estimated to exceed $8 billion, including the direct costs of medical and mental health care and the indirect costs of lost productivity.

Preventing domestic violence deserves top priority on the nation's public health agenda. Yet trying to stop domestic violence without getting to its root can be compared to pulling a dandelion out of the ground from its head: The grass looks better for a while, but the weed continues to thrive.

Theories on the Causes of Domestic Violence

The challenge of addressing the issues that live below the surface is exacerbated by the numerous theories on the underlying causes of domestic violence. For example, the biological theory suggests that violent behavior can be explained by genetics, biochemistry, and changes in brain development related to early trauma.

Some researchers believe domestic violence is rooted in individual psychopathology or dysfunctional personalities, likely shaped by early childhood experiences that lead to an inability to regulate emotions, develop trust in others, and have healthy relationships.

Another theory suggests that domestic violence is rooted in dysfunctional family interactions. Related to this is the social learning and development theory, which suggests that domestic violence is learned through exposure to behavior that is modeled, rewarded, and supported by families and cultures. In other words, if children grow up in families for whom aggression is the main type of conflict resolution, they will model that in their own relationships.

Finally, the societal structure theory holds that domestic violence reflects women's historical cultural inequality, and the reinforcement of this in political and economic arenas.

Overlap Among Theories

Significant overlap exists among the theoretical models, and experts in all camps would likely agree that domestic violence is a complex problem affected by multiple variables, the seeds of which are often sewn in childhood. For this reason, prevention efforts that seek to intervene before the seeds have an opportunity to take root—especially in higher risk populations, including females, racial minorities, and children from families living in poverty—hold the most promise.

For example, a longitudinal evaluation of a CDC-supported domestic violence prevention program called Southside Teens About Respect (STAR) in Chicago showed that awareness workshops conducted in various community locations and a school-based curriculum led to substantial improvements in participants' conflict behavior, self-ratings of relationship skills, help-seeking attitudes, and beliefs about violence in relationships.

Similar programs have begun to spring up across the country, In Oakland, Calif., the Family Violence Law Center has developed a school-based project called Relationship Abuse Prevention (RAP) that uses culturally relevant themes to teach teens about relationship and dating violence and to provide them with the tools to protect themselves.

The Center Against Domestic Violence has implemented a similar program that teaches high school students to recognize and change destructive patterns of behavior. An offshoot of that program is a middle school curriculum that teaches the self-respect and relationship skills needed to recognize and avoid various kinds of abuse. Together with increasing public and legislative intolerance of domestic violence, projects such as these can help choke the roots of domestic violence before they do damage.

> *"[In America] violence—and especially extreme, photogenic violence—is present in perpetuity, from cradle to early grave."*

American Culture Promotes Violence

Rod Liddle

Violence is part of American culture, so it should not be surprising that mass murders are commonplace in the United States, argues Rod Liddle in the following viewpoint. The United States leads the industrialized world in homicides, he maintains. Indeed, Liddle asserts, the state itself sanctions murder by executing its own citizens. Violence also permeates American entertainment, he claims. Liddle is associate editor of the Spectator, *a British magazine of news and commentary.*

As you read, consider the following questions:

1. According to Liddle, what is a "special" murder?

2. Why, in the author's view, was the 2006 murder of five girls at an Amish school not a singularity in the United States?

3. In the author's opinion, what word do social scientists use when examining the U.S. preference for "special" murders?

It was what the psychiatric services, with commendable understatement, often call a 'special' murder: obscure in its motive, repugnant in its selection of vulnerable and powerless victims, excessively brutal in its denouement. Charles C. Roberts, a milkman, marched into the West Nickel Mines Amish School in Lancaster County, Pennsylvania, at 10:30 a.m. with a nine-millimetre automatic pistol, two shotguns, a stun gun, two knives, two cans of gunpowder and buckets containing both plastic restraints and KY Jelly, a sexual lubricant.

A "Special" Murder

Roberts, who was not Amish and apparently harboured no grudge against the sect, ordered 15 boys (and a pregnant woman) out of the classroom and then began shooting; five children were killed, six more were seriously wounded. Roberts then turned the gun upon himself. His wife, speaking via a family friend, said Charles was really a quite lovely chap, all things considered, and very good with the kids—but also added that shortly before 10:30 he had called her to say he was tormented by dreams of molesting children, having sexually abused two young relatives many years before.

This fact apparently came as news to her.

There is no evidence, despite the KY Jelly, that he molested any of the schoolchildren.

So far, so singular, you might suppose.

There are madmen around and every once in a while one of them will do something particularly deranged and violent. In Britain, when things like this happen about once every ten years, we accept that it is a singularity about which not very much can be done—but we nonetheless scour our souls and our legislation, just in case we're wrong about that. The Lancaster County murders carried superficial echoes of our own Dunblane massacre of 1996, when Thomas Hamilton broke into the Scottish school and shot dead 16 young children and a teacher. Both Hamilton and Roberts were middle-aged men around whom dark intimations of paedophilia hung. In the case of Dunblane, the story occupied the front pages of our newspapers for a week or more and was the front-page lead for days; we agonised in public—how could it happen? We enacted more stringent—and possibly useless—legislation over handguns as a result, examined the efficacy of our psychiatric services, our police, our school security systems and so forth. Dunblane was sufficiently shattering to remain in the public consciousness even now—there are still websites insisting that the whole thing was a weird conspiracy or a cover-up or both, evidence perhaps of the national trauma at the time.

A Series of Murders

Will the same trauma afflict the US, away from Lancaster County? You would doubt it; ennui, perhaps, but not trauma. One day after the attack, both the *Washington Post* and the *New York Times* had relegated the story to a single column, although still on the front page (just). You doubt there will be soulsearching and legislation, except perhaps among the Amish. But this is not so much a mature response to an awful singularity—because the case of Charles C. Roberts was not remotely, however you look at it, a singularity. In the seven days before Roberts picked up his guns [on October 2, 2006], there were four similarly deranged attacks in schools across the nation: a teenage girl shot dead in Colorado, two killed in North Carolina, a teacher shot dead in Vermont, a principal killed in Wisconsin.

There have been seven such attacks, in total, in the month. The stated motives in each case were different, of course, but this should not deter us from recognising that the similarities are more than merely superficial; not simply that they hap-

America's Violent Culture

The first domain of risk for children is our American culture. As a nation, we are entertained and fascinated by violence. Physical punishment is still widely used and approved by many parents and professionals. In fact, corporal punishment is still legal in schools in many states. We are unable to regulate and protect ourselves from people toting guns, and children's rights tend to be the first to fall by the legal and legislative wayside. While perhaps not directly responsible for violence in America, society sets the stage and then closes its eyes to the tragedy.

Marjorie J. Hogan, Postgraduate Medicine, *May 15, 1999.*

pened 'in a school'. A blind and incoherent rage, for example, drove each perpetrator; it helped too that firearms were easily accessible—in the latest year for which figures are available, some 6,000 American children were expelled for carrying guns or explosives on the premises of their schools.

Some sexual motive, hidden or otherwise, was also present in most cases—but then this is pretty much a given; the profile of the indiscriminate killer of people much more vulnerable than himself almost always involves a reference to the killer's burning sexual inadequacy and dysfunction. I will not labour the point with predictable observations on the close and uncomfortable ménage a trois between sex, power and violence.

A High Rate of Murders

The US is nowhere near the top of the international table of homicide rates; that honour can be bestowed upon Colombia.

However, excluding the former Soviet states and South Africa, the US is at the top of the table for industrialised First World countries.

And more pertinent is the extraordinarily high percentage of US murders that are not motivated by robbery, narcotics, domestic argument or any of the other causes which in most countries account for 90 per cent of murders. In the US, some 39 per cent fall outside these familiar categories, and a remarkable 16 per cent are apparently 'motiveless'.

Which is where we—or the Americans, at least—should begin a bit of hand-wringing.

Examining the American penchant for 'special' murders, social scientists have a tendency to gather around the word 'brutalisation'.

A Culture of Violence

Violence—and especially extreme, photogenic violence—is present in perpetuity, from cradle to early grave. An investigation in 1998 by the US's Federal Trade Commission into the marketing and content of violent films assessed that by the age of 18 American citizens would have watched on average 200,000 acts of violence and 40,000 murders on screen.

Violence, even more than sex, has become the chief staple of mass entertainment.

And, of course, murder is sanctioned by the state. The US is the only industrialised country which will execute its citizens for 'ordinary' murders, i.e., your everyday, run-of-the-mill, beat-the-wife-to-death stuff. The death sentence has not acted as a deterrent (and, of course, could not do so in the case of nutters who intend to kill themselves after murdering other people). In a study in Oklahoma it was noted that the level of 'stranger' murders (people murdering those not known to them) substantially increased following media reports of the state execution of an unrelated murderer: this is the 'brutalisation effect'. As the social scientist Peter Morrall puts it, 'Far from preventing murders, the liquidation of a citizen by the state . . . serves to encourage some forms of homicide. Rather than identifying with the executed person . . . the would-be murderer takes his or her lead from the brutal example of legalised killing.' Murder levels are increasing, in the US and worldwide; it is expected that they will have doubled between 1990 and 2010. And where the US leads, we have a regrettable tendency to follow.

Periodical Bibliography

The following articles have been selected to supplement the diverse views presented in this chapter.

Rose Marie Berger and James Ferguson	"Mind the Gap," *Sojourners Magazine*, December 2005.
Edward J. Fink	"Violence Studies: A Growth Biz," *Broadcasting & Cable*, May 31, 2004.
Robert Grant	"Capital Punishment and Violence," *Humanist*, January–February 2004.
Carl T. Hall	"Study Finds Genetic Link to Violence," *San Francisco Chronicle*, January 23, 2007.
Issues & Controversies	"Video Games and Violence," Facts-on-File News Services, February 13, 2004.
Tom McGrath	"How the West Is Run: Do We Really Have 'No Choice' but to Join in an Addictive Cycle of Violence?" *U.S. Catholic*, November 2003.
Ted R. Miller, David T. Levy, Mark A. Cohen, et al.	"Costs of Alcohol and Drag-Involved Crime," *Prevention Science*, 2006.
Alison Motluk	"Do Games Prime Brain for Violence?" *New Scientist*, June 25, 2005.
Daniel J. Neller, Robert L. Denney, Christina A. Pietz, et al.	"Testing the Trauma Model of Violence," *Journal of Family Violence*, June 2005.
Steven Pinker	"Why Nature & Nurture Won't Go Away," *Dædalus*, Fall 2004.
John Roman	"It's a Crime What We Don't Know About Crime," *Washington Post*, July 10, 2006.
Steve Sailer	"Mapping the Unmentionable: Race and Crime," VDARE.com, February 13, 2005.

OPPOSING
VIEWPOINTS®
SERIES

CHAPTER 3

What Factors Lead to Youth Violence?

Chapter Preface

For decades activists have attacked popular music as having a negative impact on youth in the United States. Such claims have been resurrected in the early 2000s against "gangsta rap." The gangsta rap genre is an incarnation of what began as a hip-hop dance movement in mid-1970s New York City. Hip-hop and rap, terms often used interchangeably, gained broader popularity with the 1988 release of *It Takes a Nation of Millions to Hold Us Back* by Public Enemy. The group's music combines the percussive rhythm of the hip-hop dance movement and the social commentary and activism of inner-city rap poetry. Public Enemy's founder, Chuck D (Carlton Douglas Ridenhour), described rap as "the black CNN." The concern about gangsta rap, a West Coast spin-off, is its glorification of violence, sexual exploitation, and crime. The lives of some gangsta rappers are indeed violent. Rap superstars Tupac Shakur and The Notorious B.I.G., who worked for rival rap music labels, were murdered by hit men in 1996 and 1997, respectively.

The gangsta rap debate resurged recently when white shock jock Don Imus described the Rutgers University women's basketball team as "nappy-headed hos." Gangsta rap lyrics often use the term "ho" to describe women. The network canceled Imus's show, but gangsta rap's critics stepped up their demands to end the music industry's tolerance of the gangsta rap lifestyle and lyrics. Communications mogul Oprah Winfrey aired programs in which African American writers and entertainers confronted hip-hop magnates about rap lyrics. However, no conclusions were drawn concerning the impact of gangsta rap on youth violence.

Some research shows that rap lyrics do encourage violent behavior. Columnist Brent Morrison reports, "In experiments on over 500 college students . . . subjects were found to experience an increase in aggressive thoughts after listening to songs with violent lyrics." Although Morrison concedes that most well-adjusted people will not suffer any lasting harm from occasional exposure to violent lyrics, he does claim that "words do have meanings, meanings suggest thoughts, and thoughts lead to action." Claims that gangsta rap is merely a mirror of a violent society are tenuous, critics assert. According to Sheila Davis, professor of lyric writing at New York University, lyrics "are more than mere mirrors of society; they are a potent force in the shaping of it." In fact, she argues, "Popular songs provide the primary 'equipment for living' for America's youth." Unfortunately, gangsta rap critics reason, the equipment that gangsta rap lyrics provide dwells on, romanticizes, and offers an uncritical mirror for violence.

Gangsta rap's defenders insist that research shows no direct link between rap lyrics and youth violence. Based on her summary of the research, criminal justice professor Becky L. Tatum asserts, "We cannot conclude with any degree of certainty that violent and sexually explicit rap lyrics lead impressionable youths to antisocial, criminal and delinquent behavior." Reacting to the assault on gangsta rap, rapper David Banner (Levell Crump) argues that gangsta rap is no more violent than other forms of American pop culture. "People go to NASCAR [National Association for Stock Car Racing] because they want to see somebody crash. They want to see *The Departed*, with people blowing each other's heads off—that's cool, that's trendy," Banner asserts. "Gangsta rap," he claims, "is just a reflection of America. America is sick. There's so many other things we should be complaining about."

The debate over the influence of gangsta rap on youth violence is a familiar one. Violent media are often the target of critics who fear its influence on America's youth. The authors in the following chapter debate other factors believed to contribute to youth violence.

"Exposure to violent media increases feelings of hostility, thoughts about aggression, suspicions about the motives of others."

Violent Video Games and Aggressive Behavior in Children Are Linked

Elizabeth K. Carll

In the following testimony, Elizabeth K. Carll expresses the rationale behind the American Psychological Association (APA) Resolution on Violence in Video Games and Interactive Media. She asserts that research spanning several decades supports a link between violent video games and aggressive behavior in young people. Carll explains that violent video games, in part because of their repetitive nature and the player's identification with violent characters, are more likely than other media to lead to aggressive behavior. She calls for further research on the effects of violent media and more detailed warning labels to help parents decide which video games are appropriate for their children. In addition to chairing the Interactive Media Committee for the

Elizabeth K. Carll, "Violent Video Games: Rehearsing Aggression," *The Chronicle of Higher Education*, vol. 53.45, July 13, 2007. Copyright © 2007 by The Chronicle of Higher Education. Reproduced by permission of the author.

APA's Media Psychology division, Elizabeth Carll is a clinical psychologist and the author of Violence in Our Lives: Impact on Workplace, Home, and Community.

As you read, consider the following question:

1. In what ways can video games play a positive role in the lives of young people, according to Carll?

2. What are the four qualities that Carll lists that make video games and interactive media different from passive media such as film and television?

3. What is the difference, in the author's view, between video games that show negative consequences for violent acts and those that don't?

Thank you, Mr. Chairman [Senator Sam Brownback], for initiating this important hearing on violence in videogames. I am Dr. Elizabeth Carll, the chair of the Interactive Media Committee of the Media Psychology Division of the American Psychological Association (APA). The effects of media violence on children has been a career long interest with the adoption of the APA Resolution on Violence in Video Games and Interactive Media being one of the initiatives when I served as the president of the Media Division of APA. I am also a psychologist in private practice in Long Island, New York, and have worked with children, teens, and families for more than 25 years. The APA is pleased to participate in today's hearing and thanks Sen. Brownback for his important work on issues surrounding media and children.

The Interactive Media Committee was formed to facilitate the implementation of the recommendations of the Resolution on Violence in Video Games and Interactive Media, adopted by APA in August 2005, which I will be discussing. APA's Media Psychology Division spearheaded the adoption of the APA Resolution with the recognition that there is often a disconnect between research, legislation and implementation of useful recommendations at the community level.

It may be of interest for the Committee to be aware that, as a result of the APA Resolution on Violence in Video Games, a formal dialogue with the Electronic Software Ratings Board (ESRB) has begun to discuss ways in which the current ratings system may be improved.

It is also important to emphasize that electronic media plays an important role in the emotional development, social behavior and intellectual functioning of children and youth. There are many video games that are very helpful for children to facilitate medical treatment, increase learning, and promote pro-social behavior. However, there are also video games that include aggression, violence and sexualized violence that may have a negative impact on children. It is this group of video games that I will be discussing today.

Many of the issues that I will be discussing today were of concern when I first testified at the 1999 New York State legislature's hearings on the effects of violence in interactive media on children and discussed the unique characteristics of video games. However, what has changed since that time has been the rapid growth in the body of research that continues to point to the detrimental effects of violence in video games and interactive media on children, as well as the increasing public concern regarding this issue.

What are the unique characteristics of video games and interactive media vs. TV and film?

More than four decades of research have revealed that TV violence has a strong influence on the aggressive behavior of children and youth. Exposure to violent media increases feelings of hostility, thoughts about aggression, suspicions about the motives of others and demonstrates violence as a method to deal with conflict.

However, video games and interactive media have certain qualities that are distinct from passive media, (i.e., TV and film). For instance, video games:

- Require active participation enabling rehearsal and practice of violent acts, which enhances learning;

- Include frequent repetition of acts of violence as part of winning the game, which enhances learning;

- Reward game players for simulated acts of violence, which enhances learning. Often the winner of the game is the one who kills and destroys the most; and,

- Enables the identification of the participant with a violent character while playing video games, which enhances learning. Therefore, this practice, repetition, identification with a violent character and being rewarded for numerous acts of violence may intensify learning of violence. With the development of more sophisticated interactive media, the implications for violent content are of further concern.

This is due to the intensification of more realistic experiences, which may be even more conducive to increasing aggressive behavior as compared to passively watching violence on TV and in films.

Effects of Exposure to Violence

What are the effects of exposure of children to violence in video games?

A comprehensive analysis of violence in interactive video game research suggests exposure increases aggressive behavior, aggressive thoughts, angry feelings, physiological arousal and decreases helpful behavior.

Studies further suggest that sexualized violence in the media has been linked to increases in violence towards women, the acceptance of rape myth and anti-women attitudes.

Research also suggests that the most popular video games contain aggressive and violent content. Girls and women, boys and men, and minorities are depicted in exaggerated stereotypical ways. Sexual aggression against women, including assault, rape, and murder, is depicted as humorous and is glamorized and rewarded.

What are some of the concerns regarding the current rating system for video games?

Efforts to improve the rating system for video games and interactive media would be a first step in providing additional helpful information as to the content of video games. Currently, the labels are very general and more content specificity is needed for parents to make more informed decisions about the video games their children play. For example, are there only a few depictions of violence or is it a main theme? What types of violence are depicted—sports violence, war violence, sexual violence (such as rape and murder) or random thrill kill violence? Is violence linked with negative social consequences or rewarded? The scientific community should be involved in the development of a more accurate rating system to better inform parents and consumers.

Recommendations from the APA Resolution on Violence in Video Games and Interactive Media

- Advocate for funding to support research on the effects of violence in video games and interactive media on children, adolescents, and young adults. APA supports the Children and Media Research Advancement Act (CAMRA) to amend the Public Health Service Act to authorize funding to establish a program on children and the media within the Centers for Disease Control and Prevention to study the role and impact of electronic media in the development of children.

- Teach media literacy to children so they will have the ability to critically evaluate interactive media. This needs to involve educating teachers, parents and caregivers.

- Encourage the entertainment industry to link violent behaviors with negative social consequences. Showing violence without realistic consequences teaches children that violence is an effective means of resolving conflict. Whereas, seeing pain and suffering as a consequence can inhibit aggressive behavior.

- Develop and disseminate a content-based rating system that more accurately reflects the content of video games and interactive media and encourages the distribution and use of the rating system by the industry, parents, caregivers and educational organizations. The complete text of the APA Resolution on Violence in Video Games and Interactive Media is available at http://www.apa.org/pi/cyf/violence_in _videogames_interactive_media.pdf.

> *"The current body of research is unable to support the argument that the fantasy violence of games leads to real-life violence."*

The Link Between Violent Video Games and Youth Violence Is Unproven

Cheryl K. Olson

Researchers generally agree that there is no clear link between violent video games and real-life violence, argues Cheryl K. Olson in the following viewpoint. The research that does report such a link has several limitations, she claims. For example, Olson asserts, the definitions of aggression and violence are often unclear—some research does not distinguish aggressive play from aggression with the intent to harm. Moreover, she maintains, the conditions that test video game play are nothing like the way young people play games in real life. Olson is a professor of psychiatry at the Harvard Medical School Center for Mental Health and Media.

Cheryl K. Olson, "Media Violence Research and Youth Violence Data: Why Do They Conflict?" *Academic Psychiatry*, vol. 28, Summer 2004, pp. 144–49. Copyright © 2004 Academic Psychiatry. Reproduced by permission.

As you read, consider the following questions:

1. What examples does Olson provide of the American tradition of blaming corruption of youth on violent mass media?
2. While school violence is rare, what does the author say has dramatically increased?
3. In the author's opinion, what are the strongest predictors of youth violence?

It's almost an American tradition to blame the corruption of youth on violent mass media, from the lurid "half-dime" novels of the 19th century to 1930s gangster films and 1950s horror/crime comics. In 1972, a report to the U.S. Surgeon General addressed then-growing concerns about violent television. Its authors pondered how television content and programming practices could be changed to reduce the risk of increasing aggression without causing other social harms. They concluded: "The state of present knowledge does not permit an agreed answer."

Violent video games are the most recent medium to be decried by researchers, politicians, and the popular press as contributing to society's ills. In particular, they were implicated in a series of notorious shootings. . . .

School Shootings and Video Games

In response to the outcry that followed deadly shootings in Colorado, Oregon, Kentucky, and Arkansas, the U.S. Secret Service and the U.S. Department of Education began a study called the Safe School Initiative. This involved an intensive review of the 37 incidents of "targeted" school violence, aimed at a specific person, group, type (such as "jocks" or "geeks"), or at an entire school, that took place between 1974 and 2000. The goal was to look for commonalities and create a profile of potential attackers in order to prevent future tragedies.

The conclusion: There was no useful profile. Along with male gender, the most common shared trait was a history of suicide attempts or suicidal thoughts, often with a documented history of extreme depressed feelings. If all schools instituted programs to identify and refer depressed and suicidal youth, more would receive treatment and promising futures could be saved. But using those methods to detect potential killers would result in overwhelming numbers of false positives and the stigmatization of thousands.

Moreover, there is no evidence that targeted violence has increased in America's schools. While such attacks have occurred in the past, they were and are extremely rare events. The odds that a child will die in school through murder or suicide are less than one in one million. What *has* dramatically increased is our exposure to local and national news about the "recent trend" in school shootings. Research has shown that crime-saturated local and national television news reports increase viewers' perception of both personal and societal risk, regardless of actual danger.

The Role of News Coverage

Constant news coverage leaves the impression that youthful crime is increasing. Some have referred to a "wave of violence gripping America's youth," fueled by exposure to violent media. Using data supplied to the FBI [Federal Bureau of Investigation] by local law enforcement agencies, the U.S. Office of Juvenile Justice and Delinquency Prevention reported that the rate of juvenile arrests increased in the late 1980s, peaking in 1994. At the time, this seemed to be a worrisome trend, but it proved to be an anomaly. Juvenile arrests declined in each of the next 7 years. Between 1994 and 2001, arrests for murder, forcible rape, robbery, and aggravated assaults fell 44%, resulting in the lowest juvenile arrest rate for violent crimes since 1983. Murder arrests, which reached a high of 3,800 in 1993, fell to 1,400 in 2001.

The True Roots of Youth Violence

Contrary to popular belief, the origin of youth violence doesn't rest in the Mushroom Kingdom [a location in a Super Mario Bros. video game] or radiate from secret devices lodged in the Playstation 2.

The U.S. Surgeon General's 2001 report states that the strongest risk factor for school shootings and other violent acts is not media exposure, but mental stability and quality of home life. These statements have yet to change.

The deep roots of violence are buried in layers of neglect, traumatic childhood and substandard supervision.

Colin McLafferty, America's Intelligence Wire, *November 15, 2006.*

Interestingly, the sharp temporary rise in juvenile murders from 1983 to 1993 has been attributed to a rapid rise in gun use, concentrated among black male adolescents. We have no evidence that black male adolescents' use of violent media differed significantly from that of other young people, though there is ample evidence that as a group, they have greater exposure to other risk factors for violence. And what of juvenile arrests for property crimes? In 2001, these achieved their lowest level in over 30 years. In other words, there's no indication that violence rose in lockstep with the spread of violent games. Of course, this is not proof of lack of harm.

Could violent media have played some role in the rare but horrifying mass murders in our schools? This can't be ruled out, but evidence is scant. According to the Secret Service review, one in eight perpetrators showed some interest in violent video games, one-fourth in violent movies, and one-fourth in violent books, but there was no obvious pattern. Instead of interactive games, their interactive medium of choice was pen and paper. Thirty-seven percent expressed violent thoughts and imagery through poems, essays, and journal entries. . . .

Video Game Research and Public Policy

How has this spurt in electronic game play affected our youth? Along with the Washington, D.C. snipers and school shooters, several academic studies (primarily experiments) have received broad coverage in the popular media and are cited by the press and some advocacy groups as evidence that video games create dangerous, aggressive thoughts, feelings, and behaviors. Local, state, and federal legislation, including criminal penalties for selling or renting certain games to minors, have been introduced based on these studies, as have private lawsuits.

Many of these studies provide useful insights into the potential for harm (and sometimes benefit) from violent interactive games. But problems arise when the customary discussion of limitations falls by the wayside. Ideas are taken out of context and repeated in the media echo chamber, creating a false sense of certainty. Here are some of the limitations of current studies as a basis for policy making, with illustrative examples.

Vague Definitions of Aggression

Some researchers use "aggression" and "violence" almost interchangeably, implying that one inevitably leads to the other. Aggressive play that follows exposure to games or cartoons containing violence is not distinguished from aggressive behavior intended to harm. Aggressive thoughts, feelings, and behaviors may be presented as equivalent in importance and treated as valid surrogates for real-life violence, with the assumption that reducing these factors will reduce harm. The muddled terminology and unspoken assumptions can undermine the credibility of studies. After all, most parents of whining toddlers have occasional aggressive thoughts and feelings, but that's a far cry from actual child abuse.

Use of Violent Media Is Not Put Into Context with Other Known Contributors to Aggression or Violence

[Convicted Washington, D.C.-area sniper] Lee Malvo, for example, had a history of antisocial and criminal behavior. He reportedly hunted and killed perhaps 20 cats with a slingshot and marbles. Compared to playing violent video games, animal torture is both more unusual and directly related to harming humans. According to public health and juvenile justice research, the strongest childhood predictors of youth violence are involvement in crime (not necessarily violent crime), male gender, illegal substance use, physical aggressiveness, family poverty, and antisocial parents. As children grow older, peer relationships become important predictors: associating with antisocial or delinquent peers, gang membership, and lack of ties with prosocial peers and groups.

A final problem with using aggression as a surrogate for violence is that most children who are aggressive or engage in antisocial behavior do not grow up to be violent adolescents or adults, and most violent adolescents were not notably aggressive as children.

Test Conditions That Are Difficult to Generalize to the Real World

Experimental settings are not only artificial, but turn game play into game "work." Subjects may have only 10 minutes to learn and play a game before results are measured and cannot choose when to start or stop playing. Most experiments involve a single game exposure, which cannot reasonably represent the effects of playing an array of games in real life. Additionally, young people commonly play games with others. In the Kaiser Family Foundation survey, virtually all children played their video games with friends, siblings, or other relatives. (By contrast, the majority of computer games were played alone, although some children played with a friend in the room or with someone over the Internet.) Effects of the social context of games, be they positive or negative, have received little attention to date.

Small, Nonrandom, or Nonrepresentative Samples

This is another barrier to broad generalization of research results. While it is not uncommon to recruit college undergraduates in psychology courses for experimental studies, those students differ in numerous ways from the typical young American teen—the population of greatest interest to most researchers and policy makers. Other studies use samples that are very narrow in age or geography (e.g., 10- and 11-year-old Flemish children).

A Blinkered View of Causality

Some (but not all) experimental studies have found that aggressive thoughts or behavior increase after playing a particular video game. It has been postulated that experimental studies prove causality by ruling out other plausible explanations. In the real world, however, this could be a very complex relationship. That is, aggressive children may seek out violent games, and violent games may reinforce aggressive behavior. This may be a two-way relationship or the result of other factors such as lack of parental supervision or connection. Additionally, effects of moderating variables, such as the nature and context of violence in a given game, or subject age or developmental stage are often not considered.

Study Findings Are Combined in Ways Not Appropriate for Policy Use

"Meta-analysis" and related techniques, for example, may be used to merge study findings for a more robust result. A 2004 meta-analysis of the effects of playing violent video games combined studies with subjects of varying age and gender who were exposed to different types and amounts of game violence in a variety of environments (experiments and correlational studies), with varying outcomes—a range of behavioral, cognitive, affective, and arousal measures. Results were represented only in terms of average effect size. Given the different study types, exposures, populations, and outcome measures, this goes well beyond the prohibition against "comparing apples and oranges" in meta-analyses.

Again, however, the primary problem is the way these findings are interpreted. The size and representativeness of study samples were not considered in assessing study quality, and the outcome of concern—real-world violence or related harm—was never directly studied. Despite this, the results were viewed as important evidence that violent game exposure leads to major societal harm.

Current Thinking on Game Violence Effects

The research community is sharply divided on whether violent games are harmful, and if so, for whom and to what degree. Several well-regarded reviews have concluded that the current body of research is unable to support the argument that the fantasy violence of games leads to real-life violence—although this could change as evidence accumulates or games become more realistic.

In an appendix to its chapter on risk factors, the Surgeon General's 2001 report on youth violence reviewed effects of exposure to violent media. The report noted that there is evidence for a small to moderate short-term increase in physically and verbally aggressive behavior. However, the sum of findings from cross-sectional, experimental, and longitudinal studies "suggest that media violence has a relatively small impact on violence" and that "the impact of video games on violent behavior remains to be determined." . . .

We might take a lesson from America's history of media hysteria. It's time to move beyond blanket condemnations and frightening anecdotes and focus on developing targeted educational and policy interventions based on solid data. As with the entertainment media of earlier generations, we may look back on some of today's games with nostalgia, and our grandchildren may wonder what the fuss was about.

"Gang members' violent offense rates are up to seven times higher than the violent crime rates of adolescents who are not in gangs."

Gang Membership Increases Youth Violence

James C. Howell

Youth who are gang members are more likely to commit serious violent offenses than those who are not, claims James C. Howell in the following viewpoint. In fact, Howell asserts, in Los Angeles and Chicago, youth gangs are responsible for over half of the cities' homicides. Moreover, he maintains, the violent criminal activity of gang members tends to last long after they leave the gang. The costs of gang violence, Howell argues, are significant, and smaller communities that suspect a gang problem should act quickly. Howell is a senior research associate with the National Youth Gang Center.

As you read, consider the following questions:

1. According to Howell, what size cities report more gangs and gang members?

2. Where are reports of gang-related homicides concentrated, in the author's view?

James C. Howell, "The Impact of Gangs on Communities," *NYGC Bulletin*, August 2006. Reproduced by permission.

3. In the author's opinion, what are some of the ways
   youth gangs impact communities?

The impact of gangs is notably worse in the more densely
populated areas—those with populations of 50,000 or
more. Although this is not a new discovery, the National Youth
Gang Survey (NYGS) data reported here begins to paint a picture of the relative seriousness of gang problems in areas with
greater populations. On each of the criteria examined, gang
problems are far greater in cities with over 50,000 in population than in less-populated areas. More specifically, cities with
populations greater than 100,000 report noticeably more gangs
and gang members. But the very largest cities (with populations of 250,000 and above) typically report more than 30
gangs, more than 1,000 members, and far more gang-related
homicides than less-populated cities. . . .

The Impact of Youth Gang Members'
Criminal Activity

The following findings come mainly from studies of gang
member subsamples that have been embedded in several longitudinal studies of large, representative samples of children
and adolescents in three large U.S. cities (Rochester, New York;
Denver, Colorado; and Seattle, Washington) and in Montreal,
Canada. Comparative studies of these urban samples in which
the criminal activity of gang members in the samples is compared with the criminal involvement of nongang youth are
very revealing.

A comparison of the criminal acts among these two groups
of youngsters clearly shows that gang members living in high-
crime areas are responsible for far more than their share of all
self-reported violent offenses committed by the entire sample
during the adolescent years. Rochester gang members (30% of
the sample) self-reported committing 68% of all adolescent
violent offenses; in Seattle, gang members (15% of the sample)

self-reported committing 85% of adolescent robberies; and in Denver, gang members (14% of the sample) self-reported committing 79% of all serious violent adolescent offenses. In the Montreal study, gang members had four times more court appearances at age 15 and 7 times more at age 17.

Second, survey research has consistently demonstrated that youth are significantly more criminally active during periods of active gang membership, particularly in serious and violent offenses. This finding has been noted as "one of the most robust and consistent observations in criminological research." During periods of active gang membership, the Rochester gang members were responsible for, on average, four times as many offenses as their share of the total study population would suggest.

Third, gang members in the adolescent samples committed more serious crimes. In general, gang members' violent offense rates are up to seven times higher than the violent crime rates of adolescents who are not in gangs, or stated otherwise, there is a high degree of overlap between gang membership and serious violent and chronic juvenile offending. In the Rochester adolescent sample, two-thirds (66%) of the chronic violent offenders were gang members. In comparison with single-year gang members, multiple-year members have much higher serious and violent offense rates.

Fourth, the influence of gang membership on deliquency and violence is long-lasting. Analyses in the Seattle, Rochester, and Denver studies show that youths commit many more serious and violent acts while they are gang members than they do after they leave the gang. Although gang members' offense rates dropped after they left the gang in all three sites, their crime rates remained fairly high. Rates of drug use and drug trafficking, the most notable exceptions to offense rate drops, remained nearly as high after individuals left gangs as when they were active gang members. . . .

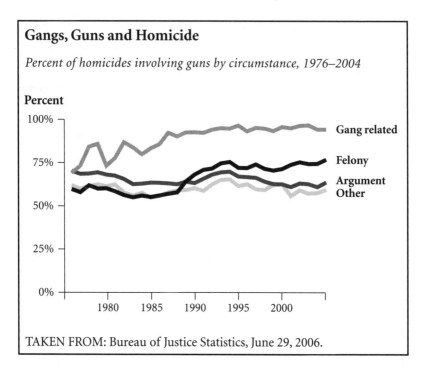

Gangs, Guns and Homicide

Percent of homicides involving guns by circumstance, 1976–2004

Percent

TAKEN FROM: Bureau of Justice Statistics, June 29, 2006.

Violent Gang Criminal Activity

Of course, homicide is the crime of greatest concern to everyone. Reports of gang-related homicides are concentrated mostly in the largest cities in the United States, where there are long-standing and persistent gang problems and a greater number of documented gang members—most of whom are identified by law enforcement as young adults. In the 2002 and 2003 National Youth Gang Surveys, nearly 4 out of 10 very large cities reported 10 or more gang homicides. However, the majority reported none or not more than one homicide.

Youth gangs are responsible for a disproportionate number of homicides. In two cities, Los Angeles and Chicago—arguably the most gang-populated cities in the United States—over half of the combined nearly 1,000 homicides reported in 2004 were attributed to gangs. Of the remaining 171 cities, approximately one-fourth of all the homicides were considered gang-related. More than 80% of gang-problem agencies, in both smaller cities and rural counties, recorded zero gang homicides. Across the United States, the number of gang homicides reported by cities with populations of 100,000 or more increased 34% from 1999 to 2003.

Jurisdictions experiencing higher levels of gang violence—evidenced by reports of multiple gang-related homicides over survey years—were significantly more likely than those experiencing no gang homicides to report that firearms were "used often" by gang members in assault crimes (47% versus 4% of the jurisdictions, respectively). Areas with longer-standing gang problems and a larger number of identified gang members—most often those with more adult-aged gang members—were also more likely to report greater firearm use by gang members in assault crimes.

Gang Entrepreneurs

Although the question of the extent to which street gangs shifted toward entrepreneurial activity in the 1980s and 1990s and the consequences of this shift are constantly debated by researchers, the reality is that gangs are often extensively involved in criminal activity. Although the proportion of all crimes committed by gang members is unknown, analyses of reported violent crimes in several cities reveal that their members often represent a large proportion of the high-rate violent offenders. Lethal violence related to gangs tends to be concentrated in the largest cities, which are mired with larger and ongoing gang problems. Frequent firearm use in assault crimes is typically reported in these larger cities.

Gang crime, however, resembles far more of a criminal smorgasbord than a main course of violence. National Youth Gang Survey respondents estimated the proportion of gang members who engaged in the following six serious and/or violent offenses in 2001: aggravated assault, robbery, burglary, motor vehicle theft, larceny/theft, and drug sales. Two clear patterns were seen. First, a large majority of agencies noted some gang member involvement in all six of the measured crimes. Second, the most frequent response was that none of these crimes were committed by a large proportion ("Most/All") of gang members within the jurisdiction, indicating considerable variability among gang members in terms of offending. Agencies that said a large proportion of gang members were involved in one or more of these offenses most often reported drug sales. A clear majority of law enforcement agencies in the NYGS report that while gang and drug problems overlap, it is typically only a subset of gang members in their jurisdiction who are actively involved in drug sales. These findings correspond with other research which finds an extensive amount of variation in the types of crimes in which gangs are involved. One noted gang researcher refers to this consistently uncovered pattern as "cafeteria-style" offending. . . .

The Impact of Gangs on Participants

Most youths who join gangs have already been involved in delinquency and drug use. Once in the gang, they are quite likely to become more actively involved in delinquency, drug use, and violence—and they are more likely to be victimized themselves. Their problems do not end here. They are at greater risk of arrest, juvenile court referral, detention, confinement in a juvenile correctional facility, and, later, imprisonment.

Gang involvement dramatically alters youngsters' life chances—particularly if they remain active in the gang for several years. Over and above embedding its members in criminal activity, the gang acts as "a powerful social network" in constraining the behavior of members, limiting access to prosocial networks, and cutting individuals off from conventional pursuits. These effects of the gang tend to produce precocious, off-time, and unsuccessful transitions that bring disorder to the life course in a cascading series of difficulties, including school dropout, early pregnancy or early impregnation, teen motherhood, and unstable employment.

This bulletin has examined the impact of youth gangs on communities in more populous cities—those with populations greater than 50,000. Some youth gangs are not actively involved in criminal acts—particularly not violent crimes. However, as one moves from small towns and rural areas to large cities, and particularly to our nation's largest cities, far more gang crime is seen. The economic impact of gangs is also far greater in these areas, with a far greater deleterious impact on communities in cities of 100,000 or more population. The very largest cities—with populations of 250,000 and above—report on average more than 30 gangs, more gang members, and far more gang-related homicides than less-populated cities.

The Impact on Communities

The disproportionate impact of gang members' criminal activity on our communities is evident in several ways. First, gang members account for more than their share of crimes. Second, youths commit more crimes during the period of active involvement in a gang than during periods before joining and after leaving a gang. Third, gang members commit more serious crimes than other groups. Fourth, the criminal involvement of youths who remain in a gang for more than a year is long-lasting.

Overall, the impact of youth gangs on communities is felt in many ways. Intimidation of other youths, adults, witnesses, and business owners is not uncommon. Once the enormous numbers of homicides in Chicago and Los Angeles are factored in, more than one-fourth of all the homicides across the country are considered gang-related. Gang immigration may be a factor of greater importance than gang migration, in terms of the impact of outsiders on local gangs. The MS-13 gang [or Mara Salvatrucha, a gang whose membership numbers in the tens of thousands in the U.S., Latin America, and Spain] may be an example of this, although its numbers are likely exaggerated in the broadcast media. On the other hand, gangs in schools are likely underestimated. In general, law enforcement agencies tend to underreport gang incidents, and their estimates of the number of gangs and gang members are likely to overlook substantial numbers of students. Last, gangs tend to propel youths into a life of crime, punctuated by arrests, convictions, and periods of incarceration. The costs to society are enormous. Each assault-related gunshot injury costs the public approximately $1 million. A single adolescent criminal career of about ten years can cost taxpayers between $1.7 and $2.3 million.

Regardless of population size, any community that senses that it is experiencing a youth gang problem needs to undertake a thorough, objective, and comprehensive assessment. This is the important first step before considering a response.

> *"In some case, the exact reasons behind a threat remain nebulous. But other times ... bullying has played a key factor."*

Bullying Is a Key Factor in Threats of Youth Violence

Cindy Horswell

In the following viewpoint, Houston Chronicle *staff writer Cindy Horswell maintains that bullying is a key factor in school violence and threats of school violence. According to Horswell, studies show that of those student shooters who survived, two-thirds had been bullied. A school bullying problem may be difficult for teachers and school administrators to identify, she claims, because bullies are often good at concealing their behavior and students do not want to be considered "snitches." Nevertheless, she argues, adults must be vigilant and teach children that bullying should not be tolerated.*

As you read, consider the following questions:

1. What are school districts that take bullying seriously doing to prevent the problem, according to Horswell?

Cindy Horswell, "Schools Learn Bully Can Plant Seed for Tragedy," *Houston Chronicle*, March 26, 2006, p. 1. Reproduced by permission.

2. In the author's view, what frustrates school administrators about the stunning acts of violence occurring at their schools?

3. According to the U.S. Department of Education, how often are students aged twelve to eighteen bullied in a period of six months?

The white prison uniform seems to swallow the slight, 5-foot-3 frame of 19-year-old Jaysen Kettl. He looks like a child compared with the tougher, more street-wise convicts surrounding him.

Kettl, convicted of plotting to kill students and teachers at his school after being bullied, never admits to being afraid at Preston Smith Prison in West Texas. But the bravado is missing from the poem he writes about his Orange County home in East Texas:

"When will I see home? Man, I feel so all alone, I think to myself, 'Why me?' I just wanna go home and see mommy."

Taking Bullying Seriously

Kettl and a sixth-grader from Crosby, who were both ostracized and taunted at school, give rare insights into the thinking of bullied students. Because of these and other area cases, school districts are realizing that teasing and bullying are more than innocent rites of passage in the school yard.

Districts are taking bullying so seriously that many are investing in prevention programs such as a pilot project initiated by the Houston school district.

Marlene Snyder, a national training director for a bully prevention program at Clemson University, said, "Bullying is really pure abuse. When you send a child to school, you expect them to be safe, not humiliated, degraded and badgered."

At 16, Kettl was certified to stand trial as an adult and now is serving four years in prison for conspiracy to murder those he accuses of tormenting him at Vidor High School. He wrote his threats in a spiral notebook called his "death book."

The 12-year-old Crosby girl, who never had a friend and repeatedly was called "stinky," according to her classmates, wound up being sent to an alternative school for writing a "hit list" of those she wanted to die.

Both the Vidor and Crosby school districts are among at least seven districts in the region and dozens nationally that have experienced threats on their campuses.

For example, a "hit list" with the encrypted message "PTK," which meant "people to kill," was confiscated from a student in the Channelview school district. And, ominous tools for another attack—six carbon dioxide canisters and instructions on how to turn them into explosive devices—were seized from a student in the Spring Branch school district.

[In March 2006], two new investigations have been launched into possible school threats. Both involve allegations that students drew maps, one detailing where to place explosives at Dulles High School in Fort Bend County and another that labeled Channelview High School in Harris County the "new Columbine."

A Reason for Threats

The massacre at Columbine High School outside Denver on April 20, 1999, was the deadliest school shooting [to that date] on record. Two teenagers, Eric Harris and Dylan Klebold, who dressed in Goth attire and felt like misfits, went on a rampage that left 13 dead and 24 wounded before killing themselves.

School administrators now are wondering why so many threats keep surfacing in America's classrooms and are starting to look into possible causes. In some cases, the exact reasons behind a threat remain nebulous. But other times—such as in the Vidor and Crosby cases—bullying has played a key factor.

What frustrates school administrators is that stunning acts of violence are occurring at a time when a 2006 U.S. Justice Department report found teen crime has been steadily dropping. Juvenile arrests for violent crimes [2003–2006] are one-third fewer than in 1980, the report said.

But, in another study that looked specifically at school shootings, the agency reported that two-thirds of the student shooters (who remained alive to talk about it) previously had been bullied. "In those cases, the experience of bullying appeared to play a major role in motivating the attacker," the report found.

For instance, a 16-year-old who went on a rampage that left eight dead at a high school in Red Lake, Minn., [in 2005] fit the profile. School personnel described him as a loner who wore black and routinely was teased.

In November 2003, Kettl concocted a detailed plot to torture and kill at least 20 of his peers, three teachers and an administrator—then commit suicide.

School administrators say they never knew of any physical abuse, only verbal abuse that centered around Kettl's heavy-metal, Goth attire and sexual orientation.

Recalling a Different Boy

Kettl's mother, Karen, said she does not think of her son as the so-called "mastermind" behind the Vidor murder plot. Rather, she remembers a "sweet and lovable" boy who was so soft-hearted that he could not stand to see his grandfather shoot a possum that had become a nuisance.

He also was bright, participating in the gifted and talented program until the eighth grade. His complaints of being "picked on" began after he left the gifted program.

But he never revealed the full extent to his mother, only occasionally acknowledging that someone had tripped him or called him a name, she said. His schoolwork also began to de-

The Role of Bullying in School Violence

- In over 2/3 of the cases [of school violence], the attackers felt persecuted, bullied, threatened, attacked, or injured by others prior to the incident.

- A number of attackers had experienced bullying and harassment that was longstanding and severe. In those cases, the experience of bullying appeared to play a major role in motivating the attack at school.

United States Secret Service Safe School Initiative, October 2000.

teriorate, and he misbehaved in class to the point that he was forced to repeat the ninth grade.

At that time, Kettl said, he asked his mother to move him to a different school. Unfortunately, his mother, a bank teller, said she didn't take him seriously, thinking it was "just more high school drama."

A few months later, in November 2003, authorities received a tip that Kettl was trying to obtain a gun, and the plot was uncovered. Authorities confiscated a knife, chains and a hammer from his backpack.

Kettl remembers how he once yearned to be a part of the crowd he later plotted to kill.

That was during elementary school, he said, before the elite group shunned him. "They didn't say anything bad to me at first," he said. "They would just get quiet whenever I came around. Or if they got together to go some place, they wouldn't tell me about it, or if I tried to sit by them, they would say they were saving that seat."

Soon, he decided, "If they don't want me in their group, then I don't want to be there."

A Group of Outcasts

He drifted to a group of students who considered themselves outcasts. Like them, his dress became flamboyant and Goth, all black clothing, black nail polish, dog collars and chains. At the same time, he declared himself a homosexual and delved into heavy metal music and Satanism.

But being different from the other school cliques drew a kind of attention that he didn't like. He tells of being relentlessly badgered and called names while at same time being shoved, pushed and tripped.

Vidor Principal Lyn Hancock describes Kettl as a "provocative victim."

"(Kettl) would complain of being picked on about his sexual orientation. We would take action and tell them to quit doing it," Hancock said. "But those he accused of being the bullies said he had come on to them more than once, especially some football players."

"I don't think it's right for other kids to bully. But at the same time, self-expression (his dress and behavior) can be taken to extreme. He knew the attention he was getting from that," said Krispin Walker, assistant district attorney for Orange County.

Kettl denies flirting with male athletes.

Prezetta White, who taught the class in Crosby where the sixth-grade girl wrote the "hit list," said bullies are clever at concealing what they do, and often the bullied child hates to be a snitch.

"We can only address what we observe. That makes it really hard," she said.

Before scribbling the word "kill" beside a list of 15 names in April, the Crosby sixth-grader said she never made a friend at school. Her name was withheld because she's a juvenile.

"One day, a kid said he'd be my friend. But he didn't. They never keep their promise," said the 12-year-old, glancing at her lap during an interview at her home.

Most students treated her as if she had a force field around her, repelling anyone who got close, she said. Then, after she was treated for lice, she said, students acted as if she were the "diseased girl" and would never let her touch them.

Classmates admitted the 12-year-old girl had grown somewhat "mean" after being repeatedly called "stinky" because she sometimes smelled or wore clothes that were stained and mismatched.

"Teachers would tell the kids to shut up, sit down and leave me alone," recalled the girl. "But they never did, until I just popped like a balloon."

She would never reveal exactly what set her off the day she wrote the list. But one classmate, Samantha Bliss, who hated the incessant teasing, said that was the first day anyone saw the 12-year-old blink back tears.

The list was confiscated and the sixth-grader was sent to alternative school.

A Multipronged Approach

Bullying remains a widespread problem in America's schools. The U.S. Department of Education estimates at least 7 percent of the nation's students ages 12 to 18 have been bullied in the past six months.

To curb bullying, a $213,000 criminal justice grant is being used to fund the Oiweus Bully Prevention Program being tested in four Houston Independent School District [HISD] campuses. It is a multipronged approach that includes a survey to assess the extent of the problem, awareness training for teachers and students, counseling and disciplinary consequences for those who bully.

The key is training everyone on a campus to recognize bullying, which ranges from verbal abuse at the lunch table or in a text message to physically harming or shunning another student, said Rebecca Killern, spokeswoman for Depelchin Children's Center, which provides counselors to HISD.

Michael Dorn, of Macon, Ga., who secretly armed himself after being tormented by schoolmates, authored a popular book, *Weakfish—Bullying through the Eyes of a Child*, to show the serious consequences of bullying.

"We need to make our kids understand what they should and should not tolerate," he said.

> *"The rise in youth violence has followed a phenomenon [called] peer orientation."*

Parenting by Peers Explains Youth Violence

Gabor Maté

Youth violence is due in part to the increasing number of children who are parented by their peers, argues Gabor Maté in the following viewpoint. In many cases economic pressures have forced both parents to work, and a child's peers must fill the void, Maté claims. Unfortunately, he maintains, without adult attachments children do not learn mature responses to frustration, and some act out violently. When fitting in with peers becomes more important than adopting adult values, preaching is futile, Maté asserts. Only reattaching young people to the adult world will prevent further violence, he concludes. Maté, a physician, is author of Hold on to Your Kids: Why Parents Matter.

As you read, consider the following questions:

1. According to Maté, what is the engine of aggression?
2. How does the author define frustration?

Gabor Maté, "Are Violent Teens Suffering 'The Rage of the Unparented'?" *Toronto (Ontario) Globe & Mail*, December 18, 2004, p. F7. Reproduced by permission of the author.

3. In the author's opinion, what does the culture of cool disguise?

Recent news should alarm all but the most complacent observers of today's youth scene. In Toronto, two teenagers have been stabbed to death by their peers, one just outside his own home as he tried to prevent some party-crashers from entering. Also in Toronto, three adolescents are on trial for the killing of a 12-year-old boy, the younger brother of one of the accused. The police officer who arrested two of them testified that, on being apprehended, they "seemed unconcerned . . . they seemed, uh, cold."

A Current of Aggression

Such events, still shocking if no longer unusual, bespeak a deep current of aggression in present-day youth culture and also an emotional detachment that has drained many young people of healthy human reactions.

The killings, beatings and bullying reported by the media represent only the tip of the iceberg. Aggression takes many other forms: Violent and dismissing language—"dissing"—is a widespread manifestation.

Less common but rapidly burgeoning is violence directed against the self, as in self-inflicted knife wounds or cigarette burns. One expert on self-harm speaks of kids getting together in "cut-of-the-month" clubs. "Our school is known for cutting," a Toronto teenager told *The Medical Post*, with a nonchalant demeanour.

Looking for Answers

What are the sources of the aggression and of the emotional shutdown? Why would young people carry potentially lethal weapons, let alone use them on each other or on themselves?

We need to look beyond facile explanations that blame parental permissiveness or a failure of moral teaching or even

What Kids Need

Experts at the National Academy of Sciences say they know why people [who grow up in dire circumstances] succeed. They've compiled a list of what children need—at home, at school, in the community—to be successful in life. This is the secret to preventing teen pregnancy, drug abuse, unemployment and youth violence, the academy says.

Kids need:

- To feel physically and psychologically safe and secure.

- Surroundings and programs that provide structure and support for their developmental needs.

- The ability to develop supportive relationships with their peers, family members and other adults.

- Opportunities to belong and participate in their peer groups, families and the larger community.

- Programs that promote positive social skills.

- To feel that their opinions matter and that they can make a difference.

- Opportunities to build skills and competency in and outside of school.

- Support from family, school and community.

Stephanie Walton and Elizabeth Gaines,
State Legislatures,
December 2006.

the glamorization of hostility by the entertainment industry. We need to look at the lives of today's children and adolescents and, above all, at what's missing in their lives.

The engine of aggression is frustration. Behind every violent act, word or feeling is pent-up frustration, unrecognized, undeclared but powerful. The adolescent erupting in hostile speech or behaviour either against himself or others has no clue about the nature of his frustration or its basic causes. The immediate target is incidental.

The young man trying to protect his home did not create the violence that killed him. The knife wielders most likely had no personal hatred toward him; perhaps they did not even know him. Their murderous frustration when he barred their entrance welled up from they knew not where.

Frustration is the primitive human response to not getting one's way, especially to not having one's essential needs satisfied.

The Rage of the Unparented

Violence is a measure of immaturity, endemic in our teen population. And immaturity has the same root as the bitter frustration that accompanies it—the unmet emotional requirements of youth deprived of nurturing adult contact. American poet and social critic Robert Bly has aptly referred to "the rage of the unparented."

The rise in youth violence has followed a phenomenon that Vancouver [British Columbia, Canada] developmental psychologist Gordon Neufeld calls peer orientation. Peer-oriented kids look not to adults, but to each other for the satisfaction of their emotional needs and for cues on to how to be, how to look and how to act.

Peer orientation is the result of an unprecedented social breakdown: the erosion of the attachment nexus in which child development ought to take place. We no longer live in villages, tribes, communities, neighbourhoods where adults mentor and raise children. The extended family is, for many kids, geographically or emotionally distant. The nuclear family is itself under extreme stress, as indicated by high divorce rates.

Economic pressures for both parents to work deprive children of the active presence of adult connections for much of the day, a lack our ill-funded and ill-conceived daycare system is unable to compensate for.

Into this void steps the peer group, with disastrous results. "Kids were never meant to nurture one another or to be role models for one another," Dr. Neufeld says. "They are not up to the task. It's the immature leading the undeveloped."

Children Parenting Each Other

Children relying on each other are unavoidably frustrated. Worse, in order to become accepted, they must become "cool." Cool is the absence of emotion, the denial of vulnerability. Cool means the shutting down of emotion, or at least the pretense of shutdown, a false sophistication characterized by invulnerability.

The aggressive gang ethic of inner-city ghetto youth now dictates the cultural style of middle-class young people across North America. The culture of cool disguises massive dissatisfaction and fear. Frightened children are masquerading as self-sufficient adults.

Peer orientation is rife among our youth. Those most affected are at greatest risk for violence against others, or for self-harm. The young knife-wielder is deathly afraid, primarily of his own vulnerability. Devoid of adult attachments that would give him safety, he affects a false machismo. When frustrated, he strikes.

The ones most embittered act out their rage in deliberate and potentially deadly attacks on others. Yet other children are so emotionally benumbed that to feel anything, they wound themselves.

Adult values are meaningless to the peer-oriented; only fitting in with the peer group matters. Adults, howsoever well-intentioned or well-qualified, are powerless to guide them. That's why there is no solution in anti-violence programs or moral preaching.

The current emphasis on moral education and behaviour modification is misguided. Peer orientation has overturned the natural order of things.

Our children will heed our leadership only if we can reattach them to us.

The young of any species, humans especially, belong under the protective wings of adults. Youth's frustration and rage will be resolved only if we succeed in restoring children's attachments to the adult world.

All of us adults—in our homes and in all our institutions, from daycare and kindergarten upward at all levels of education—must hold the emotional nurturance of children as the highest value.

We must reclaim our kids from relying on each other.

Periodical Bibliography

The following articles have been selected to supplement the diverse views presented in this chapter.

Earnestine Bennett-Johnson	"The Root of School Violence: Causes and Recommendations for a Plan of Action," *College Student Journal*, June 2004.
Lyn Boulter	"Family—School Connection and School Violence Prevention," *Negro Educational Review*, January 2004.
Kathy Christie	"Chasing the Bullies Away," *Phi Delta Kappan*, June 2005.
Gregory K. Fritz	"Predicting Violence in Adolescents," *Brown University Child and Adolescent Behavior Letter*, August 2004.
Sarah Glazer	"Video Games," *CQ Researcher*, November 10, 2006.
John Greenya	"Bullying," *CQ Researcher*, February 4, 2005.
David Healy, Andrew Herxheimer, and David B. Menkes	"Antidepressants and Violence: Problems at the Interface of Medicine and Law," *PloS Medicine*, September 2006.
Jaana Juvenon	"Myths and Facts About Bullying in Schools: Effective Interventions Depend upon Debunking Long-Held Misconceptions," *Behavioral Health Management*, March–April 2005.
Robert MacMillan	"A Replayable Debate on Game Violence," *Washington Post*, August 18, 2005.
Benjamin Radford	"Reality Check on Video Game Violence," *Skeptical Inquirer*, December 4, 2005.
William Triplett	"Gang Crisis," *CQ Researcher*, May 14, 2004.
Stephanie Walton and Elizabeth Gaines	"What Kids Need," *State Legislatures*, December 2006.

OPPOSING
VIEWPOINTS®
SERIES

CHAPTER 4

How Should Society Respond to Violence?

Chapter Preface

A recurrent question in the debate over what policies will best reduce violence is whether such policies violate people's civil liberties. Few analysts dispute that gangs are a serious nationwide problem. "Gang violence is an attack not only on individuals, but also on our communities. It stops mothers from allowing their children to play outside. It prevents the elderly from taking walks in their neighborhoods. It creates an environment of fear," Senator Dianne Feinstein asserts. What commentators do dispute is what policies will best address the problem. One tool the justice system uses to reduce illegal activities in gang-infested communities is to track gang members in computer databases. While law enforcement authorities claim these gang-tracking databases help coordinate efforts to reduce criminal gang activities, others argue that these databases unnecessarily harass citizens, particularly minorities, who have committed no crimes.

One of the most well-known gang-tracking databases was developed in California. In 1997 then-Governor Pete Wilson implemented a statewide gang-tracking program called Cal-Gang, a master database of gang members gathered from over 150 law enforcement agencies throughout the state. CalGang included the names of almost a quarter of a million people and that number continues to grow. CalGang's success, as reported by California law enforcement officials, has inspired many states nationwide to implement their own databases. To use the system, gang investigators enter information they have about a suspect, such as descriptions and location of tattoos and known gang associates. The CalGang database responds with a list of matches. Cisco Systems, the creator of the secure network on which the database is run, maintains that Cal-Gang is responsible for hundreds of arrests and has helped resolve countless crimes. The database can also determine which communities have the greatest law enforcement needs. According to Wes McBride, president and founder of the California Gang Investigators Association, "The ability to produce accurate numbers about gang-related investigations, arrests, and prosecutions makes it easier for the department to get the funding it needs."

Civil libertarians oppose gang-tracking databases for several reasons. One reason is that the criteria for inclusion in the database are so broad and sweeping that many innocent youth who are not gang members are included. Human rights journalist Nina Siegal describes some of the criteria for inclusion: "A person is a gang member or affiliate if that person 'wears colors or clothing indicating affiliation.' Another criterion legitimates guilt-by-association: A person is a gang member or affiliate if that person 'is present in a photograph with other gang affiliates.'" These criteria, critics claim, make it difficult to avoid being placed in the database. Those living in gang-ridden areas would find it difficult to avoid "hanging around" with gang members, and many young, minority males would be included simply because they wear gang-style clothing.

Complicating the problem is that few safeguards exist to prevent being falsely identified as a gang member. According to law professors Linda S. Beres and Thomas D. Griffith, "Lists are secret; access is denied to the public. Individuals have no right to know that they have been placed on a list." Indeed, they argue, "an individual may be entered on a gang database even if he has never been arrested or suspected of a crime. Once entered into a database, it seldom is possible for individuals to get their names removed." The vague criteria and the secrecy of the process, critics conclude, unnecessarily target innocent citizens.

Whether gang-tracking databases violate civil liberties remains controversial. In the following chapter, authors debate the necessity and impact of other policies designed to reduce violence.

> "[Gun control laws in Canada, Austra-
> lia, and the United Kingdom] have
> been so effectively enforced that gun-
> related death rates in those nations pale
> compared to those in the U.S."

Gun Control Laws Reduce Violent Crime

Juliet A. Leftwich

Gun control laws in other Western nations reduce violent crime, argues Juliet A. Leftwich in the following viewpoint. Arguments that gun control laws increase violence in these nations are flawed, she claims, as statistics cited to support such claims include nonviolent crime and do not include homicide. Indeed, she argues, the United States, which has by comparison little gun control, has a much higher homicide rate. If U.S. gun laws had fewer loopholes, Leftwich reasons, such laws might have a greater impact on violent crime. Leftwich is senior counsel of Legal Community Against Violence.

As you read, consider the following questions:

1. Why does the International Crime Victims Survey not include homicide, according to Leftwich?

Juliet A. Leftwich, "Pro-Gun Logic Is Wrong on the Facts," *The Recorder*, September 22, 2006. Copyright © 2006 American Lawyer Media L.P. Reproduced by permission.

2. What has been the impact of laws that require background checks on prospective gun purchasers, in the author's view?

3. What did the 2004 National Academy of Sciences report reveal about studies of defensive gun use?

Guns kill more than 30,000 people every year in this country—an average of 82 deaths each day—and injure more than 65,000 others. Despite these undisputable statistics, the basic premise of [retired law professor and gun control opponent] Don Kates' Sept. 1 [2006] article [in *Recorder*] "The Laws that Misfire," is that guns are good, and more guns are even better. He argues that violent crime rates have skyrocketed in countries which strictly regulate guns, that firearm laws in the United States are ineffective and that guns are much more likely to be used in self-defense than by criminals committing crimes. Kates contends that "more guns don't mean more death, and fewer guns don't mean less death."

Distorting the Facts

The problem with Kates' claims is that they belie the facts. Kates asserts, for example, that Canada, Australia and the United Kingdom, countries which restrict civilian handgun possession, have "the highest violent-crime rates in the Western world—more than double ours." Although Kates cites no authority for this statement in his article, his amicus curiae brief in *Parker v. District of Columbia* (before the D.C. Circuit U.S. Court of Appeals), cites an analysis of the 2000 International Crime Victims Surveys to support a similar claim.

Significantly, however, those surveys are not limited to violent crime. In fact, the International Crime Victims Surveys necessarily exclude the most violent crime—homicide—for the simple reason that homicide victims are not available to respond to a survey.

Once homicide rates are brought back into the equation, the picture changes dramatically. According to the FBI, the

U.S. homicide rate in 2004 was 5.5 per 100,000. In the same year, the homicide rate in Canada, in contrast, was 2.0 (Canadian Centre for Justice Statistics); in Australia and England/Wales it was 1.5 (Australian Bureau of Statistics, U.K. Research Development and Statistics Directorate). Thus, the homicide rate in the U.S. is many times higher than in these countries, and Kates is simply wrong when he claims that their "violent crime" rates are "more than double ours."

Restricting Access to Firearms

Kates is also wrong when he claims that laws restricting access to firearms in Canada, Australia and the United Kingdom are "unenforceable." On the contrary, it is because these laws have been so effectively enforced that gun-related death rates in those nations pale compared to those in the U.S.

According to "The Global Gun Epidemic: From Saturday Night Specials to AK-47s" (2006), the 2001/2002 rates of firearm death per 100,000 for the countries in question are as follows: U.S.: 10.27; Canada: 2.6; Australia: 1.68; and England/Wales: .38.

When one focuses on children, the comparison of international statistics is even more disturbing. According to the U.S. Centers for Disease Control and Prevention, the overall firearm-related death rate among U.S. children under the age of 15 is nearly 12 times higher than that among children in 25 other industrialized nations combined. This statistic is not surprising when one considers that Americans own far more civilian firearms—particularly handguns—than people in other industrialized nations.

Kates rejects the "quasi-religious belief that more guns (particularly handguns) mean more violence and death, and, concomitantly, fewer guns mean fewer deaths." Yet this is precisely what the empirical evidence shows. As discussed by David Hemenway, director of Harvard's Injury Control Research Center, in his book *Private Guns, Public Health* (2004), numerous studies have found that having a gun in the home is associated with an increased risk of unintentional firearm injury, suicide and homicide.

Kates contends there is no evidence that American gun laws reduce violent crime, suicide or gun accidents, relying on a 2004 report of the National Academy of Sciences. That report, however, does not suggest that legislation is an ineffective means to address gun violence. On the contrary, the thrust of the report is that additional research is needed to identify which particular policies are most likely to stem firearm-related violence and crime.

Existing research does show, however, that our nation's gun laws have had a positive impact. For example, according to the U.S. Department of Justice, the Brady Handgun Violence Prevention Act of 1993, which requires firearms dealers to conduct background checks on prospective gun purchasers, has prevented the sale of firearms to more than 1 million prohibited purchasers.

Evaluating Laws with Loopholes

Of course, our federal gun laws would be much more effective if they weren't riddled with loopholes. The Brady Act, for example, only applies to firearms dealers. Private sellers (including those who sell at gun shows) have no obligation under the act to conduct background checks on prospective buyers. Thus, criminals and other prohibited purchasers can easily buy guns throughout most of the country.

In addition, firearms dealers are permitted to transfer a firearm to a purchaser if the background check has not been completed within three days. Because of these "default proceeds," the FBI is forced to request the retrieval of thousands of firearms that have been sold to ineligible persons each year.

Moreover, guns and ammunition are exempt from the federal Consumer Product Safety Act. As a result, there are no

federal health and safety standards for domestically manufactured firearms (Such standards do exist, however, for toy guns).

Finally, federal laws do not require gun owners to be licensed or handguns to be registered. Licensing laws help ensure that gun owners know how to safely operate firearms and are familiar with applicable gun laws. Registration laws facilitate efficient tracing of crime guns, and reduce illegal sales by creating gun owner accountability. In addition, background checks conducted during the registration renewal process help ensure that a gun owner has not been convicted of a felony or otherwise become ineligible to possess firearms.

The Self-Defense Claim

Kates' remaining claims are equally without merit. Kates argues that firearm ownership is desirable for purposes of self-defense, asserting that "research has shown guns are six times more often used by victims to repel criminals than by criminals committing crimes." The 2004 National Academy of Sciences report, however, found that studies of defensive gun use reached wildly different conclusions and were potentially error-ridden:

"Self-defense is an ambiguous term that involves both objective components about ownership and use and subjective features about intent," the report said. "Whether one is a defender (of oneself or others) or a perpetrator, for example, may depend on perspective. Some reports of defensive gun use may involve illegal carrying and possession, and some uses against supposed criminals may legally amount to aggravated assault."

The Handgun Ban

Kates also contends that Washington, D.C.'s handgun ban is a failed policy, ignoring a 1991 *New England Journal of Medicine* study which found a 25 percent decline in homicides committed with firearms and a 23 percent decline in suicides committed with firearms in the district after the ban was adopted. No similar reductions were observed in the number of homicides or suicides committed by other means, nor were there similar reductions in adjacent metropolitan areas.

Although firearm homicide rates in the district subsequently increased, who is to say that those rates wouldn't have been even higher without the handgun ban?

Moreover, as Kates himself points out, laws covering a single city are difficult to enforce, given the ease with which guns can cross city limits. Of course, uniform federal gun laws would be ideal, but clearly will not be enacted by this Congress, under this president [George W. Bush], given the enormous political power of the gun lobby. In fact, during President Bush's tenure, Congress has consistently acted to weaken existing federal laws, e.g., by allowing the assault weapon ban to expire and adopting legislation to grant unprecedented legal immunity to the gun industry.

Protecting the Public

Given this situation, state and local governments must act to protect the public from gun violence. Many regulatory options are available short of a complete ban on handguns. In 2001, the National Opinion Research Center of the University of Chicago found overwhelming support for a variety of rational gun laws, including those to limit handgun sales to one per person per month (69.1 percent) and to require gun buyer safety courses (87.9 percent), background checks for private gun sales (77.5 percent), and handgun registration (76.9 percent). None of these laws prevent law-abiding citizens from owning handguns for personal protection, yet they are vehemently opposed by the gun lobby.

Gun violence has reached epidemic levels in our nation. Yet many Americans have become numb to the daily reports of firearm-related death and injury, believing there is simply nothing that any of us can do to stem the bloodshed. But there is. We can cast our votes for candidates who are willing to stand up to the gun lobby and urge our lawmakers at the federal, state and local levels to adopt the common sense gun laws we need. Despite what Don Kates says, more guns are not the answer.

| *"Gun control is ineffective in reducing crime rates."*

Gun Control Laws Do Not Reduce Violent Crime

John C. Moorhouse and Brent Wanner

According to John C. Moorhouse and Brent Wanner in the following viewpoint, there is no evidence that gun control reduces violent crime. Moreover, the authors maintain, claims that weak gun control laws in neighboring states reduce the effectiveness of gun control laws remains unproven. Nevertheless, gun control laws are politically attractive because they appear to deal with the problem of violent crime, the authors assert. What should concern politicians, the authors argue, is the violation of civil liberties that gun control laws pose. Moorhouse is a professor of economics and Wanner is a graduate student at Wake Forest University.

As you read, consider the following questions:

1. What do Moorhouse and Wanner contend gun laws control, designate, and restrict?

John C. Moorhouse and Brent Wanner, "Does Gun Control Reduce Crime or Does Crime Increase Gun Control?" *Cato Journal*, vol. 26, Winter 2006, pp. 103, 106–107, 109–10, 119, 121–22. Copyright © 2006 Cato Institute. All rights reserved. Reproduced by permission.

2. What, in the authors' view, does careful analysis of gun control require?

3. What answers do the authors give to explain why gun control is ineffective?

Advocates argue that gun control laws reduce the incidence of violent crimes by reducing the prevalence of firearms. Gun laws control the types of firearms that may be purchased, designate the qualifications of those who may purchase and own a firearm, and restrict the safe storage and use of firearms. On this view, fewer guns mean less crime. Thus, there is a two-step linkage between gun control and crime rates: (1) the impact of gun control on the availability and accessibility of firearms, particularly handguns, and (2) the effect of the prevalence of guns on the commission of crimes. The direction of the effect runs from gun control to crime rates.

Conversely, because high crime rates are often cited as justifying more stringent gun control laws, high rates may generate political support for gun regulations. This suggests a causal effect running from crime rates to more stringent gun laws. But because both relationships between gun control and crime rates unfold over time, they are not simultaneously determined in the usual econometric sense. For example, crime rates in the early 1990s could be expected, *ceteris paribus* [other things being equal], to influence the stringency of gun control measures in the late 1990s. In turn, more stringent gun control in the late 1990s could be expected, *ceteris paribus*, to affect crime rates several years later. Using state-level data, this article provides estimates of these twin relationships between gun control and crime rates. . . .

A Literature Review of Gun Control Studies

In 1993, [G.] Kleck and [E.B.] Patterson surveyed the then contemporary literature on the effects of gun controls on crime rates. As part of this larger survey, the authors review

13 studies that use state data. They observe that two studies find that gun controls reduce violent crimes, two have mixed results, and nine find no reduction in crime because of gun control.

A conspicuous characteristic of early studies is the failure to include relevant control variables. . . .

Studies Find No Evidence

A number of studies from the 1970s and 1980s that do control for social and economic factors find no evidence of gun control reducing violent crime rates. Using regression analysis, state data, and a vector of social and economic variables. [D.R.] Murray concludes that "gun control laws have no significant effect on rates of violence beyond what can be attributed to background social conditions." In addition, he observes that "controlling for basic social factors, the data show that gun laws have no significant effect on access to firearms" and "differing rates of access to handguns had no significant effect on violent acts." [D.] Lester and [M.E.] Murrell did find that "states with stricter handgun laws in 1968 were shown to have lower suicide rates by firearms both in 1960 and 1970. These states also had higher suicide rates by 'other means'." According to the authors, their finding for 1960, well before the 1968 law, is troublesome because it casts doubt on any simple interpretation of the post-law 1970 results and suggests the desirability of constructing a more complete model that includes additional variables for explaining the variation in suicide rates across states. Finally, they observe, "No such effect of strict gun control laws was found for mortality from homicides by firearms." . . .

A conundrum remains. To date, those studies that use state data and find that gun control reduces crime rates appear to be seriously flawed. On the other hand, while the majority of studies using state data do not find a deterrent effect for gun control, failure to find a statistically significant relationship is not necessarily compelling evidence that none exist. Negative findings are persuasive only if the analysis is done carefully. Among other things, careful analysis requires the use of an appropriate vector of control variables. Not only does the present study control for other factors that influence crime rates, it also uses the most detailed and sophisticated index of state gun control laws extant. This approach not only allows estimating the direct effects of a state's gun control laws on crime rates within the state but also the effect of "lax gun laws" in neighboring states.

Model One: Gun Control and Crime

The comprehensive index of state gun control, used in this study, is for 1998. To test the effectiveness of gun control in reducing crime, state crime rates for 10 categories of crime along with demographic, economic, and law enforcement data are collected for 1999 and 2001. Thus, the test is whether or not gun control, as measured by the 1998 index, has an effect on crime rates one and three years later. All crime rates are regressed against the same vector of explanatory variables including the index of gun control and a spill-in effect variable. The latter variable is included because as the Open Society Institute argues, "Very strict gun laws in one state can be undermined by permissive laws in neighboring states. When adjacent jurisdictions have different levels of gun control, the weaker law becomes the common standard."

Ten regressions are estimated for 1999 and for 2001. The endogenous variables are the overall crime rate (CRT) and rates for nine specific categories of felonies labeled: Violent, Property, Murder, Rape, Robbery, Assault, Burglary, Larceny, and Vehicle. Gun control is not expected to have the same degree of influence on each of these categories of crime. For example, firearms are rarely employed in cases of larceny, burglary, or, until recently, vehicular theft. However, all the major categories of felonies are included in the study so that the re-

Gun Control Does Not Reduce Violent Crime

Real-world experience shows that adding more gun control does not reduce violent crime. Washington, D.C., has some of the nation's most restrictive gun control laws and one of the worst violent crime rates in the country. Britain, Australia and Canada have imposed sweeping gun laws in recent years, and violent crime rates have increased dramatically in each country.

In fact, imposing more gun control is worse than ineffective, because it makes it harder for people to defend themselves when the police are not there to protect them. Research shows that guns are used thousands of times each year to prevent crimes.

Paul Guppy, Seattle Post-Intelligencer, *January 16, 2007.*

sults for crimes in which firearms are typically used and those in which they are not can be compared. . . .

Looking at the Data

Using state-level data and that for the District of Columbia, this study estimates both the impact of gun control on crime rates and the influence of crime rates on gun control. The measure of gun control adopted here is a comprehensive index, published by the Open Society Institute, covering 30 different facets of state gun laws, enforcement effort, and the stringency of local gun ordinances. The index weights upstream measures such as gun registration more heavily than downstream measures such as safe storage laws. It also weights regulations governing handguns more heavily than those on long guns.

Using a vector of demographic, economic, and law enforcement control variables, the empirical analysis presented here provides no support for the contention that gun control reduces crime rates. In none of the regressions for the 10 categories of crime rates in 1999 and the 10 for 2001 is the measure of gun control statistically significant. The article tests another hypothesis, namely, that lax gun control laws in neighboring states undermine the effectiveness of state gun laws. It finds no support for this hypothesis. The proxy for neighboring state gun control is never significant in any of the 20 regressions estimated.

By contrast, the article provides empirical support for the idea that high crime rates generate political support for the adoption of more stringent gun controls. Moreover, there is empirical evidence that the probability of adopting more gun regulations is positively related to the proportion of Democrats in the state legislature.

Gun Control Is Ineffective

The findings of this study that gun control is ineffective in reducing crime rates are consistent with the vast majority of other studies that use state data. Nevertheless questions remain. As [M.R.] DeZee observes, "We need to concentrate our efforts on determining why existing laws are not effective." The failure to find a statistically significant negative relationship between gun control and crime rates may be because gun control is ineffective or because, as Kleck argues, the aggregation problems attendant the use of state data could mask the potential relationship. However, several statistical results from this study argue against the latter interpretation. Many of the control variable coefficients in the 1999 and 2001 crime equations are statistically significant and have the expected sign. State data do not hide the expected relationships for these variables. The regressions using cross-section data explain a reasonably high degree of variation in crime rates across states. Moreover, state data do not mask the relationship flowing from high crime rates to the subsequent adoption of gun laws. The fact remains that no careful empirical study, regardless of the type of data used, has found a negative relationship between gun control measures and crime rates.

Assuming that gun control is ineffective, the question remains—why? The answer may be twofold. One, it might be that gun control simply does not influence the behavior of criminals in their efforts to obtain and use firearms. Law abiding citizens can be expected to conform to the law and obtain permits, register guns, and enroll in firearm safety courses. By contrast, there would be no surprise if it were found that criminals regularly violate the law by purchasing guns on illegal black markets or by stealing them.

Two, contemporary gun control measures typically attempt to influence the process of purchasing firearms at the point of sale between licensed dealers and their customers. Federal background checks, and often state background checks, waiting periods, and registration, are part of the process. But guns are long-lived capital assets. The stock of privately owned firearms in the United States is large relative to annual sales. Firearms are passed down through generations of family members. They are bought and sold, traded, parted out, and given away among friends, acquaintances, and strangers. It would be difficult, if not impossible, to constrain and regulate the transfer of firearms between non-dealer private parties. Gun control, while politically attractive because it appears to "deal directly with the problem" may in fact be a blunt instrument for reducing crime. Effective gun control may entail significant unintended consequences. Government extensive and intrusive enough to regulate all private transfers of firearms would raise significant civil liberties issues.

"The guidelines deserve at least part of the credit for the lower crime rate the country is currently enjoying."

Tougher Sentencing Guidelines Reduce Violent Crime

Wall Street Journal

According to the editors of the Wall Street Journal *in the following viewpoint, tough federal sentencing guidelines have contributed to a reduction in America's crime rate. Indeed, Congress passed the guidelines in response to an American public that believed the judicial system was not tough enough on crime, the* Wall Street Journal *maintains. The January 2005 Supreme Court ruling that makes the guidelines advisory rather than mandatory, however, will likely lead to sentencing disparities that the guidelines were created to avoid, the authors assert.*

As you read, consider the following questions:

1. According to the *Wall Street Journal*, how will the process of sentencing federal criminals change as a result of the January 2005 U.S. Supreme Court decision?

2. What does the author argue is the difference between a ten-year sentence handed out before and after the guidelines?

3. In the author's view, how do federal judges view the federal sentencing guidelines?

The Supreme Court handed down its long-awaited decision on the Federal Sentencing Guidelines Wednesday. And if you thought things were confusing before, just wait. About 60,000 criminals are sentenced in federal court each year, and the process will now be more bewildering than ever.

Better legal minds than ours are describing the reasoning behind this fractured pair of 5–4 judgments as "weird," "bizarre" or (our favorite for understatement) "intellectually complicated." The bottom line is that the Court decreed that the guidelines enacted by Congress 21 years ago must be considered as merely advisory, not mandatory. Judges are no longer bound to impose sentences within the ranges set by Congress.

In evaluating the Court's ruling, it helps to remember why Congress passed the 1984 sentencing guidelines in the first place. It was an effort to impose some kind of discipline on a system that was full of disparities and which an ever larger share of the American public saw as too lenient on criminals. It wasn't unusual for a person convicted of a crime in one jurisdiction to receive a sentence years or even decades longer than someone convicted of the same crime in a more liberal one. It all depended on the disposition, not to say whim, of the judges wielding the gavels.

While Wednesday's ruling restores considerable discretion to judges, it won't take the sentencing system back in time to pre-1984—despite what some critics are claiming. For one thing, the same legislation in which Congress mandated the sentencing guidelines also abolished the parole system, which often put criminals back out on the streets after serving just a brief time in jail. Unlike 21 years ago, a criminal handed a 10-year sentence today is likely to serve something close to that amount of time. Also, in recent years Congress has set mandatory minimum sentences for a wide range of crimes, and these remain unaffected by this week's ruling.

At the same time, the ruling clearly gives judges more wiggle room, and sentences are bound to vary depending on how closely a judge decides to adhere to the guidelines. Many judges will probably feel honor bound to stick to the guidelines, and disputed sentences will be reviewed by the federal appeals courts, which are told to use a "reasonableness" standard. But this is hardly a guarantee of even-handedness. A sentence deemed "reasonable" by the Second Circuit in New York could be viewed as lenient by the conservative Fourth Circuit in Richmond, Virginia, or severe by liberals on the Ninth Circuit in San Francisco.

Judges have never liked the guidelines, which from their perspective amount to 1,800 pages of Congressional micromanagement. But somehow we think they're going to like what's coming even less. Congress is not about to sit still and accept what it sees as a power grab by the judiciary.

Hearings on the guidelines are already being discussed, and legislation could follow apace. One quick fix would be for Congress to expand the number of mandatory minimum sentences, a solution that would have the ironic effect of giving judges less flexibility in sentencing than they had before Wednesday's ruling.

The Right Balance

It didn't have to come to this. The Federal Sentencing Guidelines weren't perfect, but they struck roughly the right balance among judicial discretion, Congressional oversight and jury responsibility. The guidelines deserve at least part of the credit for the lower crime rate the country is currently enjoying. With more criminals—especially recidivists—behind bars, the rate of violent crime is now at a 30-year low. This is precisely the outcome that Congress intended when it responded to public outrage over crime by passing the guidelines.

Even the Supreme Court ruling says "the ball is now in Congress' court," which may not be such a bad thing. A national debate on the correlation between prison sentences and crime would be instructive. Some tinkering with the sentencing guidelines is overdue, and Congress might even have a good idea or two, especially as compared with this fractured Supreme Court.

> *"The trouble with trying to relate federal guidelines to violent crime is that the federal government rarely has jurisdiction over such crimes."*

Tougher Sentencing Guidelines Do Not Reduce Violent Crime

Alan Reynolds

Tough, mandatory federal sentencing guidelines do not reduce violent crime, argues Alan Reynolds in the following viewpoint. The federal government rarely has jurisdiction over violent crimes; thus using federal crime statistics to make such claims is unwarranted, he maintains. Local, not federal law enforcement agents and prosecutors arrest and put away violent criminals, Reynolds claims. Because no offense or offender is the same, sentencing guidelines should be advisory, giving judges the discretion to determine the length of sentences, he contends. Reynolds is a fellow with the Cato Institute, a libertarian think tank.

As you read, consider the following questions:

1. According to Reynolds, what crimes does federal sentencing primarily involve?

Alan Reynolds, "Judges Use Judgment," *Washington Times*, January 23, 2005. Reproduced by permission of Creators Syndicate.

2. What does the author say could be the absurd result if eliminating sentencing disparities was the primary goal?

3. In the author's opinion, how have some federal prosecutors been able to coerce pleas?

In the long-awaited [*United States v.*] *Booker* decision, the Supreme Court ruled federal judges no longer have to follow the rigid sentencing "guidelines" first adopted in 1987.

The court's bold decision was promptly derided by those inclined to equate justice with unbridled prosecutorial power and endless prison sentences.

A [January 14, 2005] *Wall Street Journal* editorial, "Sentenced to confusion," imagined "the guidelines deserve at least part of the credit for the lower crime rate the country is currently enjoying." Accompanying charts purported to relate the nation's rising prison population with the decline in violent crime.

The trouble with trying to link sentencing guidelines to the total prison population, however, is that federal guidelines only apply to federal sentences. Of the 2.2 million Americans in prison or jail at the end of 2003, only 7.8 percent were in federal prisons.

The trouble with trying to relate federal guidelines to violent crime is that the federal government rarely has jurisdiction over such crimes. Former federal prosecutor Bruce Fein has written that "countless murders have been avoided, endless rapes prevented [and] innumerable robberies thwarted" due to federal sentencing rules. But it is local cops, not federal agents, who police our streets and arrest those guilty of violent crimes. The feds are rarely involved except when national banks are robbed or the crimes occurred on federal property or crossed state lines.

Federal Sentencing Is About Drugs

Homicide, aggravated assault and kidnapping accounted for only 3.3 percent of the 180,318 in federal prisons at last count.

Robbery (of banks) accounted for only 2.6 percent of federal cases sentenced in 2002. The fact that so few federal prisoners were involved in violent crimes explains why 58 percent of federal offenders can be safely kept in minimum-security or low-security facilities. About a fifth of federal sentencing involves immigration violations, and another fifth is white-collar crime, but federal sentencing is overwhelmingly about illicit drugs.

The percentage of federal prisoners incarcerated for drug offenses jumped from 27.6 percent in 1984 to 60.7 percent by 1995, partly because the guidelines mandated long prison sentences. In a recent marijuana case in Utah, a first-time offender trapped in a federal sting was sentenced to a mandatory 55 years because he refused a plea bargain and was therefore hit with 20 counts. The guidelines pretend a gram of heroin is equivalent to a kilo of marijuana, so heroin (which is easier to flush) accounted for only 7.1 percent of federal drug busts in 2002, compared with 28.9 percent for marijuana.

Gene Healy's [2004] book, *Go Directly to Jail: The Criminalization of Almost Everything*, notes there are now more than 4,000 federal offenses on the statute books, up from 3,000 a decade ago, and "thousands more buried in the Code of Federal Regulations." Despite this rush to federalize state crimes, and to criminalize torts and regulatory infractions, drug offenders nonetheless still account for more than 54 percent of federal prisoners.

The 1,823-page *Federal Sentencing Guidelines Manual* sets "base offense levels," for everything from tax evasion to possessing an eavesdropping device. The higher the number, the more time in prison. Rolling back the mileage on a car's odometer is only a Level 6 offense (no more than 18 months). Mishandling pesticides is Level 8 but jumps to Level 24 if "knowing endangerment" was involved. "Engaging in a gambling business" is a Level 12 offense, unless done by a state government or Indian tribe. "Making an obscene phone [call] for commercial purposes" (phone sex) is a Level 12 offense but Level 16 (up to 57 months) if the call was between 6 a.m. and 11 p.m. Drug charges can reach Level 38—20 years to life.

Politicizing Sentencing

Before these supposedly brilliant guidelines existed, the *Wall Street Journal* complains, there were "disparities" in sentences. But offenses and offenders are never exactly the same, which is why we should let judges be judges. If we just wanted to eliminate disparities, everyone found guilty of any victimless nonviolent crime could simply be sentenced to 55 years.

The *Journal* thinks Congress may see the Supreme Court ruling as "a power grab by the judiciary." Most federal judges saw sentencing guidelines as a power grab by the legislative branch. As former Attorney General Ed Meese explained, "A major cause of the federalization of criminal law is the desire of some members of Congress to appear tough on crime, though they know well that crime is fought most effectively at the local level."

Delegating formidable authority to a new Sentencing Commission allowed federal politicians to politicize the sentencing process by calling on the commission, through legislation or jawboning [coercing], to impose longer and longer sentences for more and more federal offenses. Conservative members of Congress could more easily attract publicity and votes by demanding longer sentences for obscenity or drugs. Liberals could demand longer sentences for antitrust violations or despoiling the environment.

The Vanishing Right to a Trial

In the process, any right to a trial where defendants may confront accusers and must be proven guilty beyond reasonable doubt has almost vanished at the federal level.

The percentage of federal cases going to trial fell from 14.6 percent in 1991 to 2.9 percent in 2002. All but a handful of

Changing Attitudes toward Mandatory Sentencing

	1995	2001
Mandatory sentences are a good idea	55%	38%
Judges should be able to decide	38%	45%

Peter D. Hart Research Associates, Inc., 2002.

federal cases are now settled with a plea bargain and sentenced on the basis of a probation officer's report.

Strict bureaucratic sentencing rules, combined with vague federal laws and regulations, are a key reason federal prosecutors no longer have to bother proving their cases to a jury. Federal prosecutors have been able to coerce pleas by threatening that if the case goes to trial they will charge numerous vaguely defined offenses and, in many cases, "forfeit" the accused person's house, car and bank account while waiting for a trial. With the risk of facing multiple counts adding up to decades of mandatory prison time, defendants with any sense of the way this game is played have no practical choice but to plead guilty to a greatly reduced charge with a reduced sentence for "cooperation."

If a misleading letter went through the mail, for example, that could mean 30 years for "mail fraud." If hearsay evidence showed two people were involved in something (which need not be a crime), such a "conspiracy" could add five more years. Accusations of being a "racketeering influenced corrupt organization" (RICO) have been applied to everything from anti-abortion groups to a chicken company.

"Obstruction of justice" is a favorite catch-all, since any remarks short of a full confession might qualify. Section 1001 of the U.S. Code says any person otherwise innocent of any crime can be sent to federal prison for up to five years for concealing a "material fact" or making a "fraudulent" statement in a conversation with any federal official or congressional staffer investigating anything, even though the accused was not under oath and not read his or her rights. Section 1001 is one of dozens of accusations that can trigger asset forfeiture (homelessness and poverty) without trial or admission of guilt.

A Transfer of Power

As Heritage fellow Paul Rosenzweig explained, "Broad and overlapping statutes with minimum obstacles to criminalization and harsh penalties . . . induce guilty pleas and produce high conviction rates, minimizing the costs of the cumbersome jury system. . . . And in the absence of any judicial check on this legislative trend, the result is a wholesale transfer of power from elected legislative officials to prosecutors who, in many instances, are unelected and not responsible to the public."

The righteous Supreme Court decision to curb the politicization of federal sentencing, moderate prosecutorial immoderation and restore judicial wisdom to the federal bench was recently described by the *Boston Globe* as "a defeat for the U.S. Justice Department." But it was a magnificent victory for justice.

| "The Red Lake shooting reminds every-
one about the importance of zero tolerance on school campuses for weapons."

Zero-Tolerance Policies at U.S. Schools Are Necessary

Spokesman Review

High school shootings, while rare, are a reminder of the need for zero tolerance of weapons in American schools, argue the editors of the Spokesman Review *in the following viewpoint. Since school shooters can come from vastly different backgrounds, school shootings can happen in any community, the authors claim. What all school shooters have in common is their access to weapons, the authors maintain, and in addition to instituting zero tolerance policies, schools need to make parents and local media aware when weapons are found in schools.*

As you read, consider the following questions:

1. According to a November 2005 U.S. Department of Justice report, where are children more likely to be victims of nonfatal serious violent crime?

2. In the opinion of the *Spokesman Review*, what kind of planning is essential for teachers, students, and administrators?

3. In the author's view, what characteristics did the Red Lake, Minnesota, and the Columbine, Colorado, shooters have in common?

They had a metal detector at Red Lake High School in Minnesota. And most surely, the adults knew the warning signs for kids who might erupt in violent ways. They knew to worry about the isolated kids, the bullied kids, the students who flirted with life's darker sides. They knew much more than adults did that February 1996 when Barry Loukaitis opened fire in his Moses Lake school and ended forever school-safety naivete.

But the metal detectors, the security guards and all the knowledge collected over the past "Columbine decade"[so named after the school shooting in April 1999, when two students killed twelve others and a teacher before taking their own lives] did not prevent the deadly day Monday [March 21, 2005] on a northern Minnesota Indian reservation. Jeff Weise, 16, shot and killed nine others before turning a gun on himself.

The multiple-victim school shooting seemed even more jarring, because it had been awhile since the last one. There were none in 2004 and only three in 2003, and in those, only a couple of people died, as if that's any cause for consolation. The U.S. Department of Justice reported in November [2004] that violent crime in schools has continued its steady decline in recent years. Students were "more likely to be victims of nonfatal serious violent crime away from school than at school."

An Important Reminder

Still, the Red Lake shooting reminds everyone about the importance of zero tolerance on school campuses for weapons

A Place for Balanced Zero-Tolerance Policies

Evidence suggests that GFSA [Gun-Free Schools Act of 1994] and the resultant zero-tolerance policies have been effective in reducing weapon possession in school. Zero-tolerance policies have been supported by various courts, especially when the policy is tied to school safety. However, suspensions and expulsions often are a product of student behavior, school policy and, more important, application of school policy. A policy that provides written guidelines that consider several factors may provide the flexibility and defensibility to address not only dangerous students but the less dangerous as well. In other words, zero tolerance has a place—just a balanced place.

David L. Stadler, Clearing House, *November–December 2004.*

and the mandate to make public to parents and the media those times when weapons are confiscated on school property.

Most importantly, the Red Lake shooting is a reminder that worst-case scenario planning is essential for teachers, students and administrators. These school-safety plans should be rehearsed with the hope they will never be needed and with the realization that even the best plans might be thwarted by young people intent on violence in their schools.

Weise was a troubled kid who wrote and spoke in violent imagery. He lived on an Indian reservation where there was a 40 percent poverty rate and a well-documented drug problem. Yet blaming his violence on this environment is as simplistic as blaming the Columbine High School tragedy on the privileged Littleton, Colo., upbringing of Eric Harris and Dylan Klebold. Much more was going on.

The shooters did have in common white supremacist beliefs and access to weapons of human destruction. The Columbine shooters built their own bombs. Weise helped himself to his law-enforcement grandfather's stash. And they most likely had in common some mental illness. According to an April 2004 article at Slate.com, FBI [Federal Bureau of Investigation] analysts and psychologists recently concluded that Klebold was severely depressed and Harris was a psychopath, so intent on violence that "if he had lived to adulthood and developed his murderous skills for many more years, there is no telling what he could have done."

The two shootings in two very different communities remind us once again that this kind of violence crosses cultural and demographic barriers. As the Red Lake community mourns its victims, the rest of the country mourns the fresh loss of innocence that happens each time a young person acts out in such a violent and radical way.

| "The time has come to break the cycle of hijacking the memories of violent school tragedies to defend zero-tolerance injustice."

Zero-Tolerance Policies at U.S. Schools Are Unnecessary

Trent England and Steve Muscatello

While school shootings are tragic, zero-tolerance policies are not the solution, claim Trent England and Steve Muscatello in the following viewpoint. Although students who bring firearms to school should be expelled, some zero-tolerance policies have been unnecessarily expanded to include expulsion for fighting and disruptive behavior, the authors assert. Some schools have even sent young children to jail, the authors stress. Absurd zero-tolerance policies should be abandoned and replaced with policies that consider a student's intent and require probable cause, the authors conclude. England is a legal policy analyst and Muscatello is a researcher at the Heritage Foundation, a conservative think tank.

Trent England and Steve Muscatello, "Six Years After Columbine? Time for Common Sense Again," *The Heritage Foundation*, April 20, 2005. Copyright © 2005 The Heritage Foundation. All rights reserved. Reproduced by permission.

As you read, consider the following questions:

1. What do England and Muscatello claim has been one legacy of the tragic school shootings in Columbine, Colorado, and Red Lake, Minnesota?

2. What are some of the examples the authors provide of normal kids who find themselves in jail?

3. What did the Texas Education Agency find was true of a third of all students prosecuted under the state's zero-tolerance statutes?

Years have passed since Eric Harris and Dylan Klebold murdered 12 students and a teacher at Columbine High School in Littleton, Colo [in April 1999]. Barely six weeks have passed since the latest schoolhouse massacre left nine people dead at Red Lake High in Red Lake, Minn. [on March 21, 2005].

Unfortunately, one legacy of these tragedies has been the well-meaning efforts of lawmakers and school administrators to prevent "the next Columbine" or "the next Red Lake" by adopting zero-tolerance—one-strike-and-you're-out—disciplinary policies. The problem is that one strike doesn't work in baseball, and it certainly doesn't work in school.

The Guns-Free School Act of 1994 required states—and thus schools—to expel automatically students who bring firearms on to school property. Since then, zero-tolerance policies have expanded to include automatic suspensions or expulsions, even in elementary schools, for fighting, disobedience and disruptive behavior.

Even worse, some schools now skip sending kids to the principal's office and instead send them straight to jail. "Zero tolerance" has come to mean that normal kids who pull normal school pranks find themselves not on suspension but in jail.

The Zero-Tolerance Dilemma

The dilemma of zero tolerance is profound and serious. One can in no way question the motives or sincerity of those who have drawn a battle line against violence in the schools. Yet however well-meaning those policies have been, the pages of national newspapers have been littered with the wreckage of young lives changed, perhaps irrevocably, by policies whose primary aim is to send a message to more serious offenders. Nor has it been substantiated that the antisocial and violent youth who are the intended targets of zero tolerance have in any way received its message. The tragic violence that has befallen both urban and rural schools makes it incumbent upon educators to explore all available means to protect the safety of students and teachers. Yet faced with an almost complete lack of evidence that zero tolerance is among the strategies capable of accomplishing that objective, one can only hope for the development and application of more effective, less intrusive alternatives for preserving the safety of our nation's schools.

Russell J. Skiba, Indiana Education Policy Center, August 2000.

Absurd Outcomes

[In August 2004], police in Espanola, N.M., arrested Jerry Trujillo, 8, because he hit a classmate with a basketball and yelled at his teacher. When he was referred to the school counselor, Jerry, who had just begun the third grade, started crying and refused to return to class. The counselor then called the police who, she said, would confine him "until [he] changes his attitude." Thus a sobbing 8-year-old entered the criminal-justice system.

Florida is full of such "criminals." Johnnie Lee Morris, 7, of Monticello, Fla., was arrested for hitting and scratching a classmate and a teacher. In St. Petersburg, a 5-year-old girl was arrested for classroom disobedience, including kicking a teacher in the shin and breaking a candy dish. The 40-pound girl was so small, police had to use plastic ties on her wrists and chained her ankles with their handcuffs. What exactly they feared a 5-year-old might do that justified such restraints is an open question.

Tate Hobart of Visalia, Calif., seemed like your average 11-year-old. According to his mother, Dana, he was a typical sixth-grader with a few minor behavioral problems but nothing serious. He even won second place in the most recent school science fair. But on March 15, he moved into the world of big-time crime—he threatened another student with a pencil.

Tate claims he threw the pencil across the room in disgust after being threatened by the other student, then said, "You have no idea how much I wanted to use that [pencil to hurt you]." But according to Liberty Elementary School principal Rosemary Spencer, Tate held the pencil "like a shank" and threatened to harm his classmate.

We'll never know the whole story because the teacher had stepped out of the classroom. But school officials thought they knew enough. And besides, even though both sides agree that no violence transpired, the California Education Code permits serious punishment even for such a "threat" of violence. And, as principal Spencer said, "We had to do something or we could've had another Columbine or what happened in Minnesota on our hands."

Thus did Tate Hobart, a normal 11-year-old and runner-up in the science fair, spend six hours in his local jail.

Time for Common Sense

It's high time for common sense to make a comeback and for there to be zero tolerance for zero-tolerance policies. If a kid brandishes a real weapon and starts making threats, by all means leap into action. But when kids are being kids, treat them as such.

That's the idea behind a bill proposed [in 2005] in the Texas legislature by state Sen. Jon Lindsay. The bill would require administrators to consider a "student's intent or lack of intent at the time the student engaged in [forbidden] conduct." His effort has gained bipartisan support in the wake of a Texas Education Agency finding that "no probable cause" for criminal charges existed for about a third of all students prosecuted under the state's existing zero-tolerance statutes.

The answer to school violence is not to transform schools into totalitarian police states and lock up every naughty child. Zero-tolerance policies rob the rule of law of its moral authority by focusing on punishment rather than justice. Six years after Columbine, the time has come to break the cycle of hijacking the memories of violent school tragedies to defend zero-tolerance injustice.

> *"Marriage tends to protect women from domestic abuse rather than increasing it."*

Promoting Marriage Will Reduce Domestic Violence

Melissa G. Pardue and Robert Rector

Promoting marriage will protect low-income mothers from domestic abuse, argues Melissa G. Pardue and Robert Rector in the following viewpoint. Indeed, the authors claim, domestic violence is more common among low-income women who move from one unmarried relationship to another. Fears that marriage promotion programs will force low-income women to stay in abusive relationships are unwarranted, the authors assert, as these programs are geared toward young, low-income couples with young children, among whom the rate of domestic violence is extremely low. Pardue is a policy analyst and Rector is a research fellow at the Heritage Foundation, a conservative think tank.

As you read, consider the following questions:

1. What do Pardue and Rector claim are some of the effects of the decline in marriage?

Melissa G. Pardue and Robert Rector, "Reducing Domestic Violence: How the Healthy Marriage Initiative Can Help," *Backgrounder [Heritage Foundation]*, no. 1744, March 30, 2004. Copyright © 2004 The Heritage Foundation. Reproduced by permission.

2. What does the Fragile Families Survey report is the median age of women having children out of wedlock?

3. What will the Healthy Marriage Initiative program provide at-risk individuals and couples?

In the United States today, one child in three is born outside of marriage. The decline of marriage is a prominent cause of child poverty, welfare dependence, and many other social problems.

In response to these concerns, President George W. Bush has proposed [in 2004] the Healthy Marriage Initiative to promote and encourage strong marriages. The proposed program would provide $300 million annually in federal and state Temporary Assistance to Needy Families (TANF) money to state-level programs that promote marriage and marriage skills, particularly among low-income and "fragile" families. All participation in the President's marriage program would be voluntary. The program would utilize existing marriage-skills education that has proven effective in decreasing conflict—and increasing happiness and stability—among target couples.

However, critics of the President's Healthy Marriage Initiative often assert that such a program would encourage or force vulnerable women into violent and dangerous relationships. Specifically, critics argue that a substantial portion of many low-income women who would participate in the marriage program are in abusive relationships and that the program would push women into marriages with abusive men, thereby increasing the rate of domestic abuse.

Erroneous Criticisms

These arguments by opponents of the Healthy Marriage Initiative are erroneous for a number of reasons:

1. Marriage-education programs that would be funded under the President's Healthy Marriage Initiative have been shown to reduce—not increase—domestic abuse.

2. The primary target groups for the healthy marriage programs would be unmarried couples at the time of a child's birth, or young, at-risk couples prior to a child's conception. The rate of domestic abuse in these groups is extremely low— around 2 percent.

3. The prevalence of domestic abuse among low-income women is often exaggerated by the use of statistics regarding whether or not a woman has *ever* been abused in her lifetime rather than whether or not abuse is occurring within a *current* romantic relationship.

4. Critics incorrectly assume that the target population for the Healthy Marriage Initiative would be older, single mothers in the TANF program. Typically, older welfare mothers have already severed ties with the fathers of their children. Such relationships have often been dead for several years: These mothers, therefore, are not good candidates for a marriage program. Rather, healthy marriage programs would seek to improve the stability and quality of relationships for low-income women at a younger age. Couples at this stage of life—generally termed "fragile families"—have relatively good prospects for entering into healthy, stable marriages.

The rate of domestic violence among these couples is low—around 2 percent. Although the rate of current abuse suffered by *older* mothers on welfare is far higher—around 20 to 30 percent—as noted, these women would not be a target group of the Healthy Marriage Initiative.

Thus, the assertion that welfare mothers experience high rates of domestic abuse is irrelevant to an assessment of the prospects of the Healthy Marriage Initiative. By intervening at a younger age, the Healthy Marriage Initiative would seek to improve the well-being of children and to reduce future child poverty and welfare dependence.

5. Many low-income mothers are trapped in patterns of serial cohabitation, moving through a sequence of fractured, failed relationships with men. Domestic violence is most likely

to occur within this pattern of serial cohabitation. The Healthy Marriage Initiative could help prevent couples from falling prey to this destructive pattern by providing them with the knowledge and skills needed to build healthy, stable relationships. The proper time for such training is when couples are at a relatively young age—either prior to a child's conception or at the time of a child's birth—before self-defeating patterns of distrust and acrimony have developed.

By helping couples to avoid the pitfalls of serial failed relationships, the Healthy Marriage Initiative will substantially reduce, rather than increase, domestic violence. Indeed, unless couples are equipped with the skills they need to develop healthy relationships, it is difficult to imagine how the current rates of domestic violence in low-income communities can be reduced.

6. Prototype healthy marriage programs, such as the Oklahoma Marriage Initiative, have not led to increases in domestic violence. In Oklahoma, more than 14,000 individuals have received training, but not a single instance of domestic abuse linked to the program has been reported. The marriage initiative works closely with local domestic violence prevention groups, and these groups have made no complaints regarding the operation of the program. . . .

The Fragile Families Survey

The Fragile Families and Child Wellbeing Study provides the best information about the low-income couples who would be the focal point of the President's Healthy Marriage Initiative. The study, which has been conducted by a team of researchers at Princeton University's Center for Research on Child Wellbeing and Columbia University's Social Indicators Survey Center, is a joint academic survey of new parents. The study is based on a nationally representative sample of parents—both married and unmarried—at the time of a child's birth.

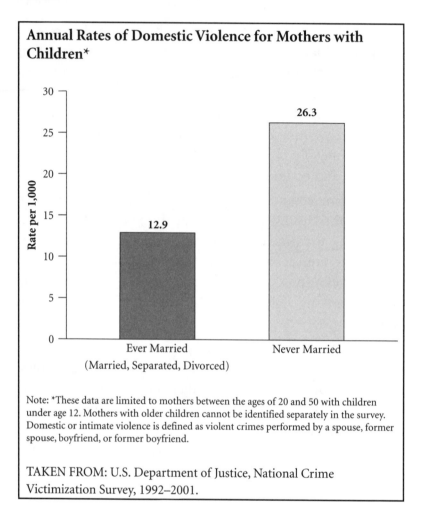

Annual Rates of Domestic Violence for Mothers with Children*

Note: *These data are limited to mothers between the ages of 20 and 50 with children under age 12. Mothers with older children cannot be identified separately in the survey. Domestic or intimate violence is defined as violent crimes performed by a spouse, former spouse, boyfriend, or former boyfriend.

TAKEN FROM: U.S. Department of Justice, National Crime Victimization Survey, 1992–2001.

Overall, the Fragile Families Survey reveals much surprising information.

- Most out-of-wedlock births occur among young adult women—not teenagers in high school. The median age for women having children out of wedlock is 22.

- Roughly half of unmarried mothers were cohabiting with the child's father at the time of the baby's birth. Nearly 75 percent were romantically involved with the father at the time of the child's birth.

- Very few unmarried fathers had drug or alcohol problems. About 98 percent of fathers had been employed during the prior year. Overall, the median annual income of the unmarried fathers was $17,500.

- Most of the unmarried couples had a strong interest in marriage: Approximately 73 percent of mothers and 88 percent of fathers believed that they had at least a 50-50 chance of marrying each other in the future.

- Among all the unmarried couples in the Fragile Families Survey, the domestic violence rate was 4 percent; however, among the roughly 75 percent of unmarried couples who were cohabiting or romantically involved, the domestic violence rate was lower—1.8 percent. These cohabiting and romantically involved couples would be the main target group of healthy-marriage programs.

Marriage as a Protective Institution

Contrary to the views of the NOW [National Organization for Women] Legal Defense Fund, marriage tends to protect women from domestic abuse rather than increasing it. In general, domestic violence is more common in cohabiting relationships than in marriages. Analysis from the National Crime Victimization Survey (NCVS), administered by the Department of Justice, also shows that mothers who are, or have been, married are far less likely to suffer from violent crime than are mothers who have never married. Specifically, data from the NCVS survey show that:

- *Marriage dramatically reduces the risk that mothers will suffer from domestic abuse.* The incidence of abuse by a spouse, boyfriend, or domestic partner is twice as high among mothers who have never been married as it is among mothers who have been married (including those who have separated or divorced).

- *Marriage dramatically reduces the prospect that mothers will suffer from violent crime in general at the hands of intimate acquaintances or of strangers.* Mothers who have never married—including those who are single and living either alone or with a boyfriend, and those who are cohabiting with their child's father—are twice as likely to be victims of violent crime as are mothers who have been married.

The pattern of cohabiting relationships among low-income women is a major factor in the increased risk for partner violence. More than half of all children in poverty come from homes with a never-married mother, and nearly two-thirds of welfare dependence occurs among households with mothers who have never married. By intervening at an early point in the lives of women, marriage programs would seek to break this cycle of cohabitation and out-of-wedlock childbearing. They would provide the skills and training needed to help women form loving, stable, and committed relationships before becoming pregnant or moving in with a violent or abusive partner.

The Healthy Marriage Initiative

The 1996 welfare reform law established national goals of reducing out-of-wedlock childbearing and increasing two-parent families. President Bush's Healthy Marriage Initiative would seek to meet these original goals of welfare reform by proposing—as part of welfare reauthorization—a new model program to promote strong marriages. His proposed program would seek to increase healthy marriage by providing at-risk individuals and couples with:

- Accurate information on the value of marriage in the lives of men, women, and children;

- Marriage-skills education that will enable couples to reduce conflict and increase the happiness and longevity of their relationships; and

- Experimental reductions in the financial penalties against marriage that are currently contained in all federal welfare programs.

All participation in the President's marriage program would be voluntary. The initiative would utilize existing marriage-skills education programs that have proven effective in decreasing conflict and increasing happiness and stability among couples. These programs have also been shown to be effective in reducing domestic violence. The pro-marriage initiative would not merely seek to increase marriage rates among target couples, but would also provide ongoing support to help at-risk couples maintain healthy marriages over time.

Marriage Initiative Would Target the Young

A well-designed marriage initiative would target participants early in their lives, when attitudes and relationships are initially being formed. Typically, such marriage-promotion programs would provide information to at-risk high school students about the long-term value of marriage. They would teach relationship skills to unmarried adult couples *before* the women become pregnant—with a focus on preventing pregnancy before couples have made a commitment to healthy marriages. The programs would also provide marriage-skills training and relationship education to unmarried couples at the "magic moment" of a child's birth and would offer marriage-skills training to low-income married couples to improve the quality of their marriage and to reduce the likelihood of divorce.

The primary focus of these marriage programs would be preventative, not reparative. They would seek to prevent the isolation and poverty of welfare mothers by intervening at an early point, *before* a pattern of broken relationships and welfare dependence has emerged. By fostering better life decisions and stronger relationship skills, marriage programs can increase child well-being and adult happiness and reduce child poverty and welfare dependence. . . .

The Benefits of Marriage

The institution of marriage has been shown to be overwhelmingly beneficial to children, adults, and society. However, for more than 50 years, government policy has discouraged marriage through the penalties inherent in the means-tested welfare system. There is now a broad consensus that this trend should be reversed and that government should promote healthy marriage. Marriage promotion has the potential to significantly decrease poverty and dependence, increase child well-being and adult happiness, and provide the safest environment for women and children.

Opponents of the President's Healthy Marriage Initiative, who claim that such a program would force women into violent and dangerous relationships by coercing or encouraging them to get married, misrepresent the goals of the program. By specifically targeting young adult men and women and at-risk high school students with information about the long-term value of marriage, marriage programs are preventative, not reparative, in nature. They seek to prevent the isolation and poverty of welfare mothers by intervening at an early point, before a pattern of broken relationships and welfare dependence has emerged. By fostering better life decisions and stronger relationship skills, marriage programs can increase the well-being of both children and adults and can reduce the likelihood of poverty, welfare dependence, and violent relationships.

> "We reject the argument that there is a
> causal relationship between marriage
> and reduced rates of domestic violence."

Promoting Marriage Will Not Reduce Domestic Violence

Family Violence Prevention Fund

In the following viewpoint the Family Violence Prevention Fund (FVPF), an organization that works to prevent domestic violence, argues that programs linking economic assistance with marriage do not reduce domestic violence. In fact, FVPF asserts, such programs put many low-income women at greater risk of abuse. Marriage promotion programs that encourage women to believe that they are harming their children if they leave their partners, make it more difficult for many to leave violent relationships, the authors claim. Marriage promotion programs fail to recognize that domestic violence is what keeps many women from economic self-sufficiency, FVPF maintains.

As you read, consider the following questions:

1. According to FVPF, what percentage of women receiving welfare have experienced physical abuse by an intimate partner?

"Testimony of the Family Violence Prevention Fund on Welfare Reform and Marriage Promotion Initiatives: Submitted to the House Ways and Means Committee," *Family Violence Prevention Fund*, February 24, 2005. Reproduced by permission.

2. What evidence does FVPF provide that marriage is anything but a panacea to poverty?

3. In the opinion of FVPF, why are marriage promotion programs not a good investment of TANF funds?

As Congress considers reauthorization of the nation's welfare program, Temporary Assistance for Needy Families (TANF), it is imperative that any welfare bill consider the particular and often urgent needs of welfare recipients who are victims of domestic violence. Research demonstrates that domestic violence is prevalent among TANF recipients and that TANF is vital in helping women to escape abuse. Congress must ensure that TANF reauthorization addresses domestic violence and enhances the safety and self-sufficiency of all TANF recipients. Given the high numbers of TANF recipients who are victims of abuse, it is imperative that the TANF program make safety a primary concern and provide families, whatever their structure, the economic resources and options they need to provide for the well-being of all family members. In order to responsibly serve all welfare recipients, and particularly those who are victims of violence, Congress should:

- Support education and training for TANF recipients;

- Improve and expand the Family Violence Option; and

- Oppose programs that encourage women to get married as a means of escaping poverty.

Rates of Domestic Violence among TANF Recipients

Congress should not consider any new TANF policies, including the proposed marriage promotion program, without serious attention to the prevalence of domestic violence in the lives of TANF recipients. Violence is not an exception to the rule for poor women; it is a reality. Studies consistently show that at least 50 to 60 percent of women receiving welfare have experienced physical abuse by an intimate partner at some point during their adult lives, compared to 22 percent of the general population. One study of two California counties, Kern and Stanislaus, found that welfare recipients had lifetime abuse rates of 80 percent and 83 percent, respectively. Young mothers, many of whom are welfare recipients, are particularly at risk for domestic and sexual violence, with one study finding that 26 percent of new mothers between the ages of 13 and 17 experienced such violence in the three months after the birth of their children. . . .

Domestic violence contributes to women's poverty and it also can create serious obstacles that prevent women, many of whom are mothers, from achieving safety and self-sufficiency. In addition to domestic violence, many welfare recipients face other barriers to employment: access to educational and job training opportunities; lack of child care; housing instability; lack of transportation; mental and physical health problems; disabilities; and substance abuse. Given this reality, battered women who receive TANF should have access to a broad range of supportive services to address the violence in their lives and the barriers to safety that they may face. Ensuring these critical services, rather than promoting marriage, should be lawmakers' priority.

The Root Causes of Women's Poverty

Common sense suggests that two incomes are better than one and that getting married is likely to move some people off of welfare. But a closer look shows that marriage is anything but a panacea to poverty. Forming a two-parent family does not guarantee greater economic security; in fact, 40 percent of families living in poverty are two-parent families.

In addition, because of death and divorce, getting married does not ensure that women will achieve economic security. Approximately 40 percent of marriages end in divorce and 12 percent end due to the husband's death. Among women currently on welfare, about 40 percent are married or were married at one time; 18.4 percent are married; 12.3 percent are separated; 8.3 percent are divorced; and about 1 percent are widows; as the Oklahoma study found, a significant number of divorces and separations are due to domestic violence. Given this, there is no indication that marriage alone would provide security, economic or otherwise, for families on welfare. Marriage promotion programs hold little hope of improving the economic situation of families who receive welfare unless they address the factors that keep women from being economically self-sufficient—child care responsibilities, lack of education and job training, and domestic violence. . . .

Marriage Does Not Reduce Domestic Violence

Proponents of marriage promotion often argue that marriage and domestic violence have an inverse relationship—that marriage causes a decrease in domestic violence. Data to support this claim includes Bureau of Justice Statistics (BJS) data drawn from the National Crime Victimization Survey (NCVS).

The NCVS tracks rates of domestic violence for three groups: never married, married, and divorced or separated women. Between 1993 and 1998, the rates of domestic violence in these three groups were as follows: 11.3 percent for never married women; 2.6 percent for married women; and 31.9 percent for divorced or separated women. Some proponents of marriage promotion argue that these numbers indicate a causal relationship between marriage and reduced rates of domestic violence because the domestic violence rates for married women are lowest. However, this misrepresents the NCVS data. First, these statistics indicate only correlation, not causation. There are many factors beyond marital status that affect domestic violence rates. For example, the age cohorts of women who fall into these three groups—never married, mar-

Violent Marriages Are a Barrier

[One] criticism of marriage promotion comes from survivors of domestic violence and their advocates. Studies consistently show that between 50% and 60%—in some studies up to 80%—of women on welfare have suffered some form of domestic violence, compared to 22% of the general population. In addition, between 3.3 and 10 million children witness domestic violence each year. Domestic violence survivors say their abuse was often a barrier to work, and many have reported being harassed or abused while at work. Most survivors needed welfare to escape the relationship and the violence. Any policy that provides incentives for women to become and stay married is in effect coercing poor women into marriage. Many women on welfare . . . say that their marriages, rather than helping them out of poverty, set up overwhelming barriers to building their own autonomous and productive lives.

Sarah Olson, Dollars & Sense, *January–February 2005.*

ried, and divorced or separated—must be taken into consideration. Young women age 16 to 24 are particularly at risk for domestic violence and this group is highly represented in the never married category, which has an 11.3 percent reported rate of domestic violence.

Second, as the BJS states: "Because the NCVS reflects a respondent's martial status at the time of the interview, it is not possible to determine whether a person was separated or divorced at the time of the victimization or whether the separation or divorce followed the violence." In other words, there is no way to know whether the 31.9 percent of divorced or separated women were victims of violence during or after marriage. Without this information, it is impossible to conclude that rates of domestic violence are actually lower for married women. In fact, it is far more likely that many divorces were prompted by violence or that violence and abuse contributed to the divorce.

Finally, it is widely accepted that reporting rates for domestic violence are low across the board, and it should be expected that married women who are experiencing violence would be less likely to report, given that they often have more at stake, such as children, family, and financial considerations. Thus, we reject the argument that there is a casual relationship between marriage and reduced rates of domestic violence. . . .

Marriage Promotion Programs May Be Dangerous

Marriage promotion programs raise myriad concerns about the health and safety of battered women and their children that must not be ignored. Given the economic vulnerability of many welfare recipients, particularly battered women, the decision to participate in a marriage promotion program may not be fully informed or optional. By stigmatizing single parents, stigmatizing divorce, or encouraging women to believe that they are harming their children if they leave their partners, these programs make it more difficult for some women to leave violent relationships or encourage them, intentionally or not, to remain with abusive partners.

In addition, participation in marriage promotion programs may be, or may be perceived to be, linked to the receipt of TANF benefits and other services. There is little doubt that financial incentives to marry or stay married would encourage women to remain in abusive relationships. For example, West Virginia's TANF program has offered a $100 incentive if the parents in a household receiving welfare get married, and the U.S. Department of Health and Human Services' own compilation of model programs for states that are developing marriage promotion programs suggests a $2,000 cash bonus for couples who marry.

No one should be pushed into making a decision that could adversely affect his or her safety and health. But the proposed TANF law actually requires states to set numerical performance goals for marriage promotion programs in their state plans. This would pressure state officials to encourage women to marry, thereby making it likely that individuals will be coerced or pressured into marriages that may not be healthy or safe.

Finally, marriage promotion programs are not a good investment of TANF funds. Scarce public funds should not be diverted from desperately needed economic supports, such as child care and job training, into questionable programs that are unlikely to help reduce poverty or increase the safety and well-being of recipients and their families. Precious TANF funds should not be spent to promote potentially dangerous marriages; they should be used for the supports and services that will help to lift all families, including battered women and their children, out of poverty.

Marriage Promotion Programs May Not Improve Child Outcomes

Marriage promotion programs, which have been touted as a way to improve outcomes for children, may in fact have the opposite effect. Battered women are not the only victims of abuse; their children are affected as well. In a national survey of more than 6,000 American families, 50 percent of the men who frequently assaulted their wives also frequently abused their children. Experts estimate that 3.3 to 10 million children witness domestic violence each year and research demonstrates that exposure to violence can have serious negative effects on children's development. . . .

Researchers found that males exposed to family conflict and violence over the years were significantly more likely than other males to have suicidal thoughts, be depressed, have emotional and behavioral problems, be drug dependent, or have post-traumatic stress disorder. Girls from violent homes had higher rates of alcohol problems and lower grades when they graduated from high school than girls who did not experience conflict or violence in their homes. These findings show that growing up in a violent home can take a terrible toll on children and teens, and can cause serious, long-lasting harm. . . .

The research on child outcomes suggests that marriage promotion programs may actually endanger children who grow up in violent homes and negatively affect their development by encouraging women to remain in violent relationships. Two-parent families are not ideal when there is violence or abuse; in fact, this kind of household can be damaging or dangerous for women and children who experience or witness violence.

Education and Training

Rather than focusing on a potentially dangerous marriage promotion program that may not lift women out of poverty or improve child outcomes, Congress should strengthen existing provisions to support women who receive TANF. TANF programs should support education and training opportunities that will help recipients find and keep well-paying jobs, with appropriate measures to protect victims of violence. There is a direct link between educational attainment and economic well-being. In 2000, only 1.2 percent of single mothers with a college degree who worked full-time year round lived in poverty. Less than eight percent of single mothers with some college working full-time lived in poverty. Clearly, education, not marriage, is the best and most direct strategy for lifting families out of poverty.

When parents have access to education, children also benefit. For example, among children whose parents work full-time and year-round: 72 percent of children whose parents do not hold a high school degree live in low-income families, compared to 42 percent of children whose parents have a high school degree, and only 16 percent of children whose parents have at least some college. Parents who have educational opportunities beyond high school have drastically improved economic outcomes and are better able to provide for their children.

In addition, Congress must understand that any increase in required work hours or state work participation rates will have a negative effect on education and training programs and may in fact prevent women from finding well-paying jobs. In welfare reauthorization, Congress must recognize that welfare recipients achieve greater economic security when they are given the opportunity to gain new skills and knowledge. Investments in education, training and work supports can both empower women to achieve economic security (which empowers families and couples as well) and strengthen marriages.

Strengthening the Family Violence Option

While most women who experience domestic violence want to work if possible, some may need help or extra time to find or keep work that will lead to self-sufficiency. In addition to strengthening education and training programs, the Family Violence Option (FVO) should be expanded to include all 50 states and to require each state to certify that it has trained caseworkers who can screen individuals for domestic and sexual violence, or that it will contract with domestic violence experts who will conduct the screenings. All states should be required to give oral and written notice to individuals who have been sanctioned or are at risk of being sanctioned that welfare program requirements may be waived if domestic or sexual violence has contributed to their non-compliance. Congress should also fund demonstration projects to develop and disseminate best practices in addressing domestic and sexual violence as a barrier to economic security.

While the FVO is not mandatory, 33 states and the District of Columbia have adopted it. Eleven other states have equivalent policies that enable violence victims to get waivers from some or all TANF requirements. Six states—Idaho, Indiana, Mississippi, Oklahoma, Virginia and Wisconsin—have no FVO or equivalent policies.

Currently, the FVO allows states to: screen for and identify victims of domestic violence; refer victims of domestic violence to appropriate services; grant "good cause" waivers to domestic violence victims when TANF requirements are harmful or unsafe; and protect the confidentiality of domestic violence victims and their children. In addition, the FVO exempts states from TANF requirements when excusing domestic violence victims who fail to meet TANF requirements results in a state's failure to meet its TANF work participation and/or 60-month limit requirements. Congress should both strengthen and expand the FVO in the next reauthorization of the TANF program.

Supporting Safety and Self-Sufficiency

Given the large numbers of TANF recipients who are victims of domestic violence, Congress must address violence as a primary concern in the lives of women and children who receive welfare. Welfare and work are powerful tools in helping battered women leave abusive relationships, particularly when women have access to supportive services such as education, job training, mental health services, and child care. In contrast, marriage promotion programs run the risk of endangering battered women and their children and do not address the root causes of poverty for families on welfare.

Welfare reauthorization must focus on meaningful and gainful employment; recipients must be allowed to gain the education and training skills necessary to finding well-paying jobs; and barriers to employment such as domestic violence must be reasonably and responsibly addressed. In contrast, the marriage promotion initiative that Congress may include in the TANF program has not been shown to reduce poverty, and it poses a threat to the safety of battered women and their children. Rather than supporting an untested and potentially dangerous marriage promotion program, TANF reauthorization should help families on welfare who are experiencing domestic violence while supporting the safety and self-sufficiency of all TANF recipients.

Periodical Bibliography

The following articles have been selected to supplement the diverse views presented in this chapter.

Bob Adams — "Gun Control Debate," *CQ Researcher*, November 12, 2004.

Roy N. Aruffo — "A 5-Year-Old in Handcuffs?" *Clinical Psychiatry News*, June 2005.

Beth Dalbey — "The Bogeyman Is Us," *Business Record*, October 23, 2006.

Michael Goldsmith — "Reconsidering the Constitutionality of Federal Sentencing Guidelines after Blakely: A Former Commissioner's Perspective," *Brigham Young University Law Review*, 2004.

Kristin A. Goss — "The Missing Movement for Gun Control," *Chronicle of Higher Education*, October 20, 2006.

Alan M. Gottlieb — "Another View: Violent Crime Rise Proves Need for Personal Protection Capability," *Sheboygan Press*, January 12, 2007.

Anita Hamilton — "Video Vigilantes: If Parents Don't Monitor Kids' Access to Violent and Sexual Games, Should the States Do It?" *Time*, January 10, 2005.

Stephen Johnson and David Muhlhausen — "No Silver Bullet for Youth Gangs," *Washington Times*, August 30, 2005.

Erica Little and Brian W. Walsh — "Federalizing 'Gang Crime' Is Counterproductive and Dangerous," *Web Memo* (Heritage Foundation), September 22, 2006.

Erik Luna — "Let Judges Do Their Job," *Philadelphia Inquirer*, August 9, 2004.

David L. Stadler — "Zero Tolerance as Public Policy: The Good, the Bad, and the Ugly," *Clearing House*, November–December 2004.

For Further Discussion

Chapter 1

1. Mary Lou Leary maintains that victims of violent crime not only suffer from the immediate impact of the crime but experience costly long-term emotional injuries. Tim Wise does not dispute the impact of violent crime but argues that exaggerating the scope of the problem leads to strict laws that do not reduce violent crime but increase the number of nonviolent offenders that are incarcerated. The authors use different types of evidence to support their claims. Is one type of evidence more persuasive than the other? Explain, citing from the viewpoints.

2. This chapter's viewpoint authors dispute the seriousness of the problem of violence in the community, in school, and in the home. They argue that the focus on crime and violence in the media and in political campaigns falsely leads people to fear that violence is a more serious problem than it is. Does the evidence and/or rhetoric used by these authors also have a common thread? Explain why or why not, citing from the viewpoints.

3. Dianne Feinstein argues that domestic violence is a serious problem that threatens American families. Stephen Baskerville asserts that labeling an assault/domestic violence is unnecessary as assault is already a crime. Those accused of assault have more legal protection than those accused of domestic violence, he claims. Do you agree that there are sufficient differences between an assault and domestic violence to warrant special protection from perpetrators of domestic violence? Explain why or why not, citing from both viewpoints.

Chapter 2

1. Several of the authors in this chapter emphasize specific factors that they believe play a major role in violence. What types of evidence are used to support each conclusion? Which types of evidence do you find most persuasive? Explain your answers, citing from the viewpoints.

2. To support his conclusion that evolution has favored violent humans, Richard Wrangham compares aggression in primate groups to similar behavior in human groups. Robert M. Sapolsky also compares primate and human behavior but cites peaceful exceptions to support his argument that evolution has sometimes favored primates and human populations that are not violent. Which do you think human societies resemble more, violent or nonviolent primates? Cite examples in the viewpoints to support your conclusions.

3. Jared Taylor and Tim Wise cite the same violent crime statistics but come to opposite conclusions. Which interpretation of the statistics do you find more persuasive? Citing the viewpoints, explain your answer.

4. Diana Mahoney cites several theories on the underlying causes of domestic violence. Which theory do you believe can best be addressed by the prevention strategies Mahoney recommends? Explain.

Chapter 3

1. Which factors that the authors in this chapter claim lead to youth violence do you believe play the greatest role in youth violence? Explain your answers, citing from the viewpoints.

2. Elizabeth K. Carll asserts that research has established a link between violent video games and youth aggression. Cheryl K. Olson counters that these studies have limitations that make it difficult to draw any conclusions about

video games and real-life violence. Which viewpoint do you find more persuasive? Explain.

3. The authors of the viewpoints in this chapter have a variety of different affiliations. Evaluate how the affiliation of each author affects that author's level of persuasiveness. Explain using material from the viewpoints.

Chapter 4

1. To support her argument that gun control laws would reduce violent crime in the United States, Juliet A. Leftwich asserts that gun control laws have reduced violent crime in other nations. John C. Moorhouse and Brent Wanner maintain, by contrast, that evidence equating gun control and violent crime reduction are flawed. Which viewpoint do you find more persuasive? Explain, citing from the texts.

2. The editors of the *Spokesman Review* claim that the fact that school shootings continue to threaten American communities demonstrates a need for zero tolerance of weapons in schools. Trent England and Steve Muscatello assert that zero-tolerance policies are an overreaction to tragic shootings. These policies, they argue, have led to absurd results. What evidence do the authors use to support their claims? Is one type of evidence more persuasive? Explain.

3. Melissa G. Pardue and Robert Rector argue that promoting marriage will protect low-income mothers from domestic violence. The Family Violence Prevention Fund maintains that programs that promote marriage will have the opposite effect, making poor women more vulnerable to abuse. Do you think Pardue and Rector's assertion that marriage promotion programs will primarily target younger women is sufficient to allay the Fund's fears that these programs will prevent women from leaving violent partners? Explain why or why not, citing from the texts.

4. What commonalities among the viewpoints on both sides of the debate can you find in this chapter? Explain, citing from the viewpoints.

Organizations to Contact

The editors have compiled the following list of organizations concerned with the issues debated in this book. The descriptions are derived from materials provided by the organizations. All have publications or information available for interested readers. The list was compiled on the date of publication of the present volume; the information provided here may change. Be aware that many organizations take several weeks or longer to respond to inquiries, so allow as much time as possible.

**American Academy of Child
and Adolescent Psychiatry (AACAP)**
3615 Wisconsin Ave. NW, Washington, DC   20016-3007
(202) 966-7300 • fax: (202) 966-2891
Web site: www.aacap.org

AACAP is a nonprofit organization that supports and advances child and adolescent psychiatry through research and the distribution of information. The academy's goal is to provide information that will remove the stigma associated with mental illnesses and assure proper treatment for children who suffer from mental or behavioral disorders due to child abuse, molestation, or other factors. AACAP publishes "Facts for Families" on a variety of issues concerning disorders that may affect children and adolescents. Titles available on its Web site include "Understanding Violent Behavior in Children and Adolescents" and "Children and Video Games: Playing with Violence."

American Coalition for Fathers and Children (ACFC)
1718 M St. NW, Ste. 187, Washington, DC   20036
(800) 978-3237 • fax: (703) 442-5313
e-mail: info@acfc.org
Web site: www.acfc.org

ACFC supports efforts to create a family law system that promotes equal rights for all parties affected by divorce and the breakup of a family. The coalition believes that the Violence Against Women Act destroys families and funds an anti-male, pro-feminist ideological agenda. ACFC publishes the quarterly newspaper, *The Liberator,* samples articles from which are available on its Web site.

American Psychological Association (APA)
Office of Public Affairs, 750 First St. NE
Washington, DC   20002-4242
(202) 336-5700
e-mail: public.affairs@apa.org
Web site: www.apa.org

This society of psychologists aims to "advance psychology as a science, as a profession, and as a means of promoting human welfare." Although the APA opposes censorship, it believes that viewing media violence can have potential dangers for children. On its Web site the APA provides access to its Adults & Children Together Against Violence program (www.actagainstviolence.apa.com), which includes information on the impact of media violence and suggestions for parents and others who care for children.

Brady Campaign to Prevent Gun Violence
1225 Eye St. NW, Ste. 1100, Washington, DC   20005
(202) 898-0792 • fax: (202) 371-9615
Web site: www.bradycampaign.org

The goal of the Brady Campaign to Prevent Gun Violence is to create a United States that is free from gun violence. The campaign works to enact and enforce sensible gun laws, regulations, and public policies through grassroots activism and increasing public awareness. The campaign publishes facts sheets, issue briefs, and special reports on its Web site, including "Kids and Guns in America" and "Domestic Violence and Guns."

Center for Successful Parenting
1508 E. Eighty-Sixth St., Indianapolis, IN   46240

e-mail: csp@onrampamerica.net
Web site: sosparents.org

Founded in 1998, the Center was created to increase awareness of the negative effects of violent media on children and move the public to action to protect children from media violence. On its Web site the Center provides news, fact sheets, and tools to help parents protect their children from the risks of media violence, including a media violence bibliography of research and articles on media violence.

Family Violence Prevention Fund

383 Rhode Island St., Ste. 304
San Francisco, CA   94103-5133
(415) 252-8900 • fax: (415) 252-8991
e-mail: info@endabuse.org
Web site: www.endabuse.org

The Family Violence Prevention Fund believes that everyone has the right to live free of violence and works to prevent violence within the home and in the community. It sponsors special education campaigns and was instrumental in lobbying Congress to enact the Violence Against Women Act. The fund publishes fact sheets, news briefs, and the *Family Violence Prevention Fund Newsletter*, recent issues of which are available on its Web site, including articles such as "Men Speak Out Against Violence."

Gun Owners of America (GOA)

8001 Forbes Place, Ste. 102, Springfield, VA   22151
(703) 321-8585 • fax: (703) 321-8408
e-mail: goamail@gunowners.org
Web site: www.gunowners.org

GOA is a nonprofit lobbying organization that defends the Second Amendment rights of gun owners. It has developed a network of attorneys to help fight court battles to protect gun owner rights. GOA also works with members of Congress, state legislators, and local citizens to protect gun ranges and local gun clubs from closure by the government. On its Web site the organization publishes fact sheets and links to op-ed articles, including "People Don't Stop Killers, People with Guns Do" and "Is Arming Teachers the Solution to School Shootings?"

Media Coalition
139 Fulton St., Ste. 302, New York, NY   10038
(212) 587-4025 • fax: (212) 587-2436
e-mail: mediacoalition@mediacoalition.org
Web site: www.mediacoalition.org

The Media Coalition defends the First Amendment right to produce and sell books, magazines, recordings, videotapes, and video games. It defends the U.S. public's right to have access to the broadest possible range of opinion and entertainment, including works considered offensive or harmful due to their violent or sexually explicit content. It opposes the government-mandated ratings system for television. On its Web site the coalition provides legislative updates and access to reports, including *Shooting the Messenger: Why Censorship Won't Stop Violence.*

National Coalition Against Domestic Violence (NCADV)
1633 Q St. NW, Ste. 210, Washington, DC   20009
(202) 745-1211
Web site: www.ncadv.org

NCADV believes that violence against women and children results from the use of force or threats to achieve and maintain control over others in intimate relationships. The coalition believes that the abuses of power in society foster battering by perpetuating conditions that condone violence against women and children. Therefore, NCADV works to change these societal conditions. The coalition publishes fact sheets and a suggested reading list, which are available on its Web site. Its newsletter, *The Grassroots Connection*, and *The Voice: A Journal of the Battered Women's Movement* are available with membership.

National Criminal Justice Reference Service (NCJRS)

PO Box 6000, Rockville, MD 20849-6000

(301) 519-5500 • fax: (301) 519-5212

e-mail: askncjrs@ncjrs.org

Web site: www.ncjrs.org

NCJRS is an agency of the U.S. Department of Justice established to prevent and reduce crime and to improve the criminal justice system. The NCJRS Web site provides access to numerous reports on crime and justice organized alphabetically, including *Domestic Violence Legislation; Gang Members and Delinquent Behavior; Teens, Crime, and the Community*; and *Violence Against Women: Identifying Risk Factors, Research in Brief.*

National Major Gang Task Force

338 S. Arlington Ave., Ste. 112, Indianapolis, IN 46219

(317) 322-0537 • fax: (317) 322-0549

e-mail: nmgtf@earthlink.net

Web site: www.nmgtf.org

This task force is an independent organization specializing in intervention, management strategies, networking, training, and information-sharing regarding gangs. It publishes reports and books, including *Juvenile Violence: A Guide to Understanding Juvenile Violence in America*, which may be purchased on its Web site.

National School Safety Center (NSSC)

4165 Thousand Oaks Blvd., Ste. 290

Westlake Village, CA 91362

(805) 373-9977 • fax: (805) 373-9277

Web site: www.nsscl.org

Affiliated with Pepperdine University, the NSSC is a nonprofit training organization created by presidential directive in 1984 to promote safe schools and to help ensure quality education for all children in the United States. The center identifies, promotes, and shares promising practices and programs. On its Web site the center makes available the handouts "Bullying in Schools: Fact Sheet Series" and "Creating Safe Schools."

National Youth Gang Center (NYGC)

PO Box 12729, Tallahassee, FL   32317
(800) 446-0912 • fax: (850) 422-3529
Web site: www.iir.com/nygc

A research program of the Institute for Intergovernmental Research, NYGC collects and analyzes information on gangs. The Center assesses the scope and characteristics of youth gang activity in the United States, develops resources, and provides training and technical assistance in support of gang suppression efforts. NYGC publications include the reports *High School Youths, Weapons, and Violence: A National Survey; Youth Gangs: An Overview*; and *The Youth Gangs, Drugs, and Violence Connection*, which are available on its Web site.

Office of Juvenile Justice and Delinquency Prevention (OJJDP)

810 Seventh St. NW, Washington, DC   20531
(202) 307-5911
Web site: http://ojjdp.ncjrs.org

The OJJDP is a Justice Department office that provides leadership, coordination, and resources on preventing juvenile delinquency and victimization. It supports states and communities in their efforts to develop and implement effective prevention and intervention programs and to improve the juvenile justice system so that it protects public safety, holds offenders accountable, and provides treatment and rehabilitative services tailored to the needs of juveniles and their families. A searchable database of articles and reports is available on its Web site.

U.S. Department of Justice

800 K St. NW, Ste. 920, Washington, DC   20530
(202) 307-6026 • fax: (202) 307-3911
Web site: www.usdoj.gov/owv

The U.S Department of Justice Office of Violence Against Women (OVW) provides federal leadership to reduce violence against women, dating violence, sexual assault, and stalking. The office also administers Violence Against Women Act grants to state, local, tribal, and nonprofit entities that respond to violence against women. OVW publications on domestic violence and teen dating violence can be found at the National Criminal Justice Reference Service Web site identified above. The OVW Web site publishes fact sheets on domestic violence and teen dating violence, the Violence Against Women Act, and related legislation such as the Violent Crime Control and Law Enforcement Act.

Bibliography of Books

Rami Benbenishty   *School Violence in Context: Culture, Neighborhood, Family, School, and Gender.* New York: Oxford University Press, 2005.

Dewey G. Cornell   *School Violence: Fears Versus Facts.* Mahwah, NJ: Lawrence Erlbaum Associates, 2006.

Elizabeth Kandel Englander   *Understanding Violence.* Mahwah, NJ: Lawrence Erlbaum Associates, 2007.

Laura L. Finley, ed.   *Encyclopedia of Juvenile Violence.* Westport, CT: Greenwood, 2007.

James Garbarino   *See Jane Hit: Why Girls Are Growing More Violent and What We Can Do About It.* New York: Penguin, 2006.

Nancy G. Guerra and Emilie Phillips Smith, eds.   *Preventing Youth Violence in a Multicultural Society.* Washington, DC: American Psychological Association, 2006.

Darnell F. Hawkins, ed.   *Violent Crime: Assessing Race and Ethnic Differences.* New York: Cambridge University Press, 2003.

David Hemenway   *Private Guns, Public Health.* Ann Arbor: University of Michigan Press, 2004.

James B. Jacobs   *Can Gun Control Work?* New York: Oxford University Press, 2002.

Steven J. Kirsh — *Children, Adolescents, and Media Violence: A Critical Look at the Research.* Thousand Oaks, CA: Sage, 2006.

Louis A. Knafla — *Violent Crime in North America.* Westport, CT: Praeger, 2003.

Richard A. Lawrence — *School Crime and Juvenile Justice.* New York: Oxford University Press, 2007.

Jack Levin — *The Violence of Hate: Confronting Racism, Anti-Semitism, and Other Forms of Bigotry.* Boston: Pearson Allyn and Bacon, 2007.

John R. Lott — *The Bias Against Guns: Why Almost Everything You've Heard About Gun Control Is Wrong.* Washington, DC: Regnery, 2003.

Paula K. Lundberg-Love and Shelly L. Marmion, eds. — *"Intimate" Violence Against Women: When Spouses, Partners, or Lovers Attack.* Westport, CT: Praeger, 2006.

John R. Lutzker, ed. — *Preventing Violence: Research and Evidence-Based Intervention Strategies.* Washington DC: American Psychological Association, 2006.

Ruth D. Peterson, Lauren J. Krivo, and John Hagan — *The Many Colors of Crime: Inequalities of Race, Ethnicity, and Crime in America.* New York: New York University Press, 2006.

Michel Prum, Bénédicte Deschamps, and Marie-Claude Barbier, eds.
Racial, Ethnic, and Homophobic Violence: Killing in the Name of Otherness. New York: Routledge-Cavendish, 2007.

Claire M. Renzetti and Raquel Kennedy Bergen, eds.
Violence Against Women. Lanham, MD: Rowman & Littlefield, 2005.

Harold Schechter
Savage Pastimes: A Cultural History of Violent Entertainment. New York: St. Martin's, 2005.

Kathy Sexton-Radek
Violence in Schools: Issues, Consequences, and Expressions. Westport, CT: Praeger, 2005.

Irving A. Spergel
Reducing Youth Gang Violence: The Little Village Gang Project in Chicago. Lanham, MD: AltaMira, 2007.

Robert J. Spitzer
The Politics of Gun Control. Washington, DC: CQ Press, 2004.

R. Murray Thomas
Violence in America's Schools: Understanding, Prevention, and Responses. Westport, CT: Praeger, 2006.

David Trend
The Myth of Media Violence: A Critical Introduction. Malden, MA: Blackwell, 2007.

Avelardo Valdez
Mexican American Girls and Gang Violence: Beyond Risk. New York: Palgrave Macmillan, 2007.

Irvin Waller

Less Law, More Order: The Truth About Reducing Crime. Westport, CT: Praeger, 2006.

Franklin E. Zimring

The Great American Crime Decline. New York: Oxford University Press, 2007.

Index